Power and Love

A Reos Partners Publication

Praise for *Power and Love*

"Adam's *Solving Tough Problems* helped me understand that all of our pressing problems—be they strategic issues inside a company or societal challenges like conflict, poverty, or climate change—require that those with a stake and the power to act come together in open dialogue to create a joint diagnosis and a deep commitment to moving forward together. In *Power and Love*, Adam goes further and deeper, into the kind of leadership that it takes to do this."

—Ravi Venkatesan, Chairman, Microsoft India

"It isn't either-or; it's both-and. In this deceptively brief and clearly written book, Adam Kahane takes us through his own learning process to a way of acting in and on the world that is both effective and caring. Intelligent, insightful, satisfying—and inspiring."

—Mary Catherine Bateson, author of *Composing a Life* and *Willing to Learn*

"Kahane is a master practitioner and thinker who knows the highs and lows of solving some of the toughest problems of social discord. *Power and Love* is both instructive and inspiring."

—Patrick Dodson, winner of the Sydney Peace Prize and Founding Chairman, Council for Aboriginal Reconciliation

"This book is a must-read for business leaders who are coming to recognize that to continue to thrive, business must join forces with interest groups, communities, and government to address the wicked sustainability challenges of our time. Kahane shows us how."

—Diane Osgood, Vice President, Business for Social Responsibility

"The cynical side of me says that Adam Kahane is unique and that it's his personality and presence that enable him to overcome conflict and create constructive resolutions to stalemates in business and society. But the hopeful side says that yes he is special but that his ideas—which he explains so ably in *Power and Love*—can be used by others. He writes not from theory but from experience—and draws out the lessons from a lifetime of fostering constructive engagement to deal with the toughest challenges."

—Esther Dyson, founder, EDventure Holdings

"This is a superb book: wise and thoughtful."

—W. Brian Arthur, External Professor, Santa Fe Institute, and author of *The Nature of Technology*

"If we are to move forward on the many challenges humanity faces, only through a symbiosis of power and love can we enable the social change we need, that both unifies and is sufficiently creative. This book offers a glimpse of what a new praxis of creative collective action might look like."
—Ged Davis, former Managing Director, World Economic Forum, and former Vice President, Royal Dutch Shell

"Reconciling extremes is the challenge of our time. Sharing insights born from working in the trenches of the world's toughest social problems, Adam Kahane calls for the extraordinary measure of embracing the wholeness of our power and our love: the hard and soft in us all. By illuminating this 'uncommon way,' Kahane's message joins the stream of the world's most profound and enduring strategic views."
—James Gimian, publisher, *Shambhala Sun*, and coauthor of *The Rules of Victory*

"Mahatma Gandhi's life was the unfolding of the deep truth of the need to change oneself if one wants to change the world. Hence his autobiography was titled *My Experiments with Truth*. Adam's story of his engagements with people in many countries, whom he was called to help in their efforts to change their worlds, is an account of his own realization of Gandhi's insight. An honest and beautifully told story."
—Arun Maira, member, Planning Commission of the Government of India

"In this evocative and beautifully written narrative, Adam Kahane shares his own journey toward a deeper and more life-affirming understanding of the relationship between love and power—both in ourselves and in the systems we work with. His real-life stories and the lessons they reveal are compelling for all of us who work with complex issues involving multiple stakeholders."
—Juanita Brown, cofounder, The World Café

"This is a courageous book. Too few of us who frequent the halls of power are willing to acknowledge the power of love. Not Adam. In this delicate and sensible book, we see a necessary dialectic, an uneasy partnership of power and love that is essential to solving the problems we face."
—Jay Ogilvy, Dean, Presidio Graduate School, and cofounder, Global Business Network

"This is a remarkable book. Kahane fuses his real experience and earned wisdom into a clear new lens through which social change practitioners and theorists can better see how expressions—and shadows—of love and power shape the outcomes of their efforts to solve complex social problems."
—Ross McMillan, President, Tides Canada

"From climate disruption to health care, from poverty to war, the range of seemingly intractable crises we face today is enough to cause despair in even the most hopeful. Yet these are the kinds of problems that Adam Kahane has grappled with around the world. In *Power and Love*, Kahane uses these experiences to explore why success in the face of complex challenges requires not just a new understanding of the problems but a new understanding of ourselves."

—Jamais Cascio, cofounder, WorldChanging.com

"Adam Kahane has mined more than two decades of practice to create a brave, concise, compelling reflection about the mistakes he has made, the lessons he has learned, and the hard-earned theory that now guides his work. *Power and Love* has a humility that is becoming and a depth that is inspiring."

—Katherine Fulton, President, Monitor Institute

"An extraordinarily insightful and powerful analysis of what it takes to lead change and to make a difference in society. Drawing on his own experiences around the world, Kahane uses his skills of acute observation and honest self-reflection to figure out how to effect deep and lasting social change—starting with oneself."

—Fields Wicker-Miurin, cofounder, Leaders' Quest

"Bringing 'power' and 'love' together in resolving the most intractable social problems is not only unusual, it may also seem unreal. Adam Kahane makes it radically mandatory."

—Njabulo Ndebele, former Vice-Chancellor, University of
Cape Town, and author of *Fine Lines from the Box*

"Adam Kahane is a change agent of the first order. His welcome and timely book will help readers refocus and strengthen their commitment and ability to effect much-needed community and societal change."

—Mari Fitzduff, Professor and Director, Masters Program in
Coexistence and Conflict, Brandeis University

"This book is written with great insight and revealing honesty. Adam is a wonderful storyteller, grounds his thinking in reality, and in this book gives us a path to making a lasting difference in the world."

—Peter Block, author of *Stewardship*, *The Answer to
How Is Yes*, and *Community*

"*Power and Love* should be read and reread by anyone seriously committed to addressing tough problems."

—Morris Rosenberg, Deputy Minister of Health, Government of Canada

"A timely book that contains clear lessons about how, why, and when systemic, participatory, and generative interventions, aimed at shaping the future, work or fail."
—Angela Wilkinson, Director of Scenario Planning and Futures Research, Institute for Science, Innovation, and Society, University of Oxford

"Effective and sustainable responses to global health challenges require business, government, and civil society to work together in partnership—but such partnerships do not easily deliver win-win-win outcomes. Kahane's thoughtful and grounded reflections on his own experiences of success and failure show us the way."
—Paulus M. Verschuren, Senior Director, Global Health Partnerships, Unilever

"As leaders in the private, public, and social sectors, we all struggle to navigate tensions. Adam Kahane points out that the polarity of power versus love underpins them all. As long as we approach this polarity with an 'either-or' filter, we will remain stuck; only when we embrace it as an 'and' can we breathe life into change. Kahane shows us how to embody this 'and' and so to lead effectively and gracefully."
—Zafer Achi, Managing Director, Middle East, McKinsey & Company

"International conflict is commonly understood by governments through the lens of realpolitik. The limitations of such a strategic analysis of power is that it does not recognize the power of human motivation. Adam Kahane's wise and insightful book addresses this by integrating the concepts of love and power."
—Gabrielle Rifkind, Director, Human Security in the Middle East Programme, Oxford Research Group

"Kahane addresses the often-neglected need to create alternative social structures in situations where power, competition, and self-interest continue even after deeply entrenched disputes have been 'settled' through conflict resolution and negotiation. Reflective and practical: a must-read."
—Charles Villa-Vicencio, former National Research Director, South African Truth and Reconciliation Commission

"This is not a book about simple solutions to complex problems; it is the tale of a twenty-year pilgrimage, one man's courageous journey into the unknown, a willingness to take on some of the world's most complex and seemingly intractable problems, at the same time working on one's own intractability. *Power and Love* is the antidote to resignation; it is about the hope and possibility that comes from committing oneself to making a difference in the world."
—Barry Oshry, author of *Seeing Systems* and *Leading Systems*

"In the four decades since Martin Luther King's death, change agents across the world have sought to ground themselves in his powerful and loving practice. Adam Kahane's book is a journey and a road map to that practice."
—Michel Gelobter, CEO, Cooler, and former President, Redefining Progress

"Adam's courageous exploration of his struggle with the paradoxes of power and love invites us into our own exploration of this crucial tension. Our capacity to deal with our toughest social challenges—even our survival as a species—depends on our learning to work skillfully with these two fundamental drives."
—Phil Cass, CEO, Columbus Medical Association

"Based on his firsthand experiences working with leaders—from across sectors, organizations, and communities, around the world—who are dealing with tough problems, Kahane's beautifully written book offers a jewel of wisdom to those who want to effect profound social change: learn to speak both the language of power and the language of love."
—Elena Díez Pinto, Executive Director, Soros Foundation–Guatemala, and former Executive Director, Visión Guatemala

"This thought-provoking book will help leaders of social change efforts undertake their challenging work more positively and powerfully."
—Bob Head, CEO, Skandia

"*Power and Love* expands and refines the analysis of *Solving Tough Problems*. A renowned practitioner of the delicate art of convening diverse and often warring stakeholders to solve intractable problems together, Kahane has a genius for extracting fundamental insights and principles from complex experiences. This small book will stimulate fresh thinking by researchers, practitioners, and policymakers everywhere who are concerned with catalyzing sustainable social change."
—L. David Brown, Senior Research Fellow, Hauser Center for Nonprofit Organizations, Harvard University

"Power pushes, love pulls. Adam Kahane understands these two fundamental forces like few hands-on practitioners of conflict resolution. *Power and Love* is that rare jewel—a manual and a sonnet."
—Robert Fuller, author of *Dignity for All, All Rise*, and *Somebodies and Nobodies*

"*Power and Love* outlines Adam's unique approach to solving problems, which enables people to make sense of their world—past, present, and future—so that they can make it better."
—Paul Hanratty, CEO, Long-Term Savings, Old Mutual plc

"Adam Kahane takes systems thinking over into systems doing. He tells us stories of how separated parts are brought—lovingly—into serving the purposes of the whole of the social order. Kahane walks his talk. He is a principled pragmatist."
—Bo Ekman, Founder and Chairman, Tällberg Foundation

"Power without love cannot sustain the long-term, coordinated effort necessary to achieve social change; love without power cannot overcome entrenched interests. Kahane's stories and his wise counsel show how we can work with these apparent opposites to create new worlds."
—Betty Sue Flowers, coauthor of *Presence* and former Director, Lyndon Baines Johnson Library and Museum

"Adam's book is an important contribution to our understanding of how to co-create new social realities."
—Otto Scharmer, Chair of the Presencing Institute and author of *Theory U*

Praise for *Solving Tough Problems*

"This breakthrough book addresses the central challenge of our time: finding a way to work together to solve the problems we have created."
—Nelson Mandela

"A seminal book. Exciting, vital, essential reading."
—Edgar H. Schein, Professor of Management Emeritus, Massachusetts Institute of Technology Sloan School of Management, and author of *Process Consultation* and *Helping*

"Our societies face really hard problems—poverty, injustice, sustainability, corruption—that are insoluble by conventional means. Conflicts of interest and profound uncertainties about the future are producing paralysis and inaction. Adam Kahane has, more than anyone, developed and successfully employed tools that enable us to create futures of shared progress and profit."
—Peter Schwartz, Chairman, Global Business Network, and author of *The Art of the Long View*

"Highly relevant to the global challenges we face today."
—Debra Dunn, Senior Vice President, Hewlett-Packard

"This book should be read by everyone who is concerned with the quality of decision making in our democracies."
—Elena Martinez, Assistant Secretary-General, United Nations

Power and Love

A THEORY AND PRACTICE OF SOCIAL CHANGE

Adam Kahane

Drawings by Jeff Barnum

Berrett–Koehler Publishers, Inc.
San Francisco
a BK Currents book

Berrett-Koehler Publishers, Inc.
235 Montgomery Street, Suite 650
San Francisco, CA 94104-2916
Tel: (415) 288-0260   Fax: (415) 362-2512   www.bkconnection.com

Ordering Information
Quantity sales. Special discounts are available on quantity purchases by corporations, associations, and others. For details, contact the "Special Sales Department" at the Berrett-Koehler address above.
Individual sales. Berrett-Koehler publications are available through most bookstores. They can also be ordered directly from Berrett-Koehler: Tel: (800) 929-2929; Fax: (802) 864-7626; www.bkconnection.com
Orders for college textbook/course adoption use. Please contact Berrett-Koehler: Tel: (800) 929-2929; Fax: (802) 864-7626.
Orders by U.S. trade bookstores and wholesalers. Please contact Ingram Publisher Services, Tel: (800) 509-4887; Fax: (800) 838-1149; E-mail: customer.service@ingram-publisherservices.com; or visit www.ingrampublisherservices.com/Ordering for details about electronic ordering.

Berrett-Koehler and the BK logo are registered trademarks of Berrett-Koehler Publishers, Inc.

Printed in the United States of America
Berrett-Koehler books are printed on long-lasting acid-free paper. When it is available, we choose paper that has been manufactured by environmentally responsible processes. These may include using trees grown in sustainable forests, incorporating recycled paper, minimizing chlorine in bleaching, or recycling the energy produced at the paper mill.

Library of Congress Cataloging-in-Publication Data
Kahane, Adam.
  Power and love : a theory and practice of social change / by Adam Kahane. — 1st ed.
      p. cm.
  Includes bibliographical references.
  ISBN 978-1-60509-304-8 (pbk.)
  1. Power (Social sciences) 2. Social interaction. 3. Social change. I. Title.
  HM1256.K34 2010
  303.48'4—dc22
                                         2009023948

First Edition
15 14 13 12 11 10   10 9 8 7 6 5 4 3

Interior design: Gopa&Ted2 Design   *Proofreader:* Henrietta Bensussen
Copy editor: Judith Brown   *Indexer:* Medea Minnich
Production: Linda Jupiter Productions

To my mother and father

"Power properly understood is nothing but the ability to achieve purpose. It is the strength required to bring about social, political, and economic change. . . . And one of the great problems of history is that the concepts of love and power have usually been contrasted as opposites—polar opposites—so that love is identified with the resignation of power, and power with the denial of love. Now we've got to get this thing right. What [we need to realize is] that power without love is reckless and abusive, and love without power is sentimental and anemic. . . . It is precisely this collision of immoral power with powerless morality which constitutes the major crisis of our time."

—MARTIN LUTHER KING JR.,
"Where Do We Go From Here?"

Contents

Preface   ix

INTRODUCTION: BEYOND WAR AND PEACE   1
Two fundamental drives   2
Our full world   4
Two pitfalls   7
An imperative   9

1: THE TWO SIDES OF POWER   11
Generative power   12
Degenerative power   15
Love is what makes power generative   26

2: THE TWO SIDES OF LOVE   29
Generative love   29
Degenerative love   38
Power is what makes love generative   50

3: THE DILEMMA OF POWER AND LOVE   53

4: FALLING   57
Improving child nutrition in India   57
How to fall   71

5: STUMBLING   75
Bridging divides in Israel   75
Building democracy in South Africa   87
How to stumble   100

6: WALKING   103
    Growing sustainable food in Europe
        and the Americas   103
    Mitigating climate change in Canada   113
    How to walk   121

CONCLUSION:
TO LEAD MEANS TO STEP FORWARD   127
    Becoming aware of both our power and our love   129
    Balancing ourselves   129
    Practicing moving fluidly   134
    Stepping forward   139

Notes   143
Bibliography   151
Acknowledgments   155
Index   160
About Reos Partners   168
About the Author and the Artist   170

Preface

*H*OW CAN WE ADDRESS our toughest challenges? How can we break through our most entangled, stuck problems? How can we create social change?

I have spent the past twenty years searching for answers to these questions. My work has been to help teams of leaders come together from across a given social system to address a particular challenge that all of them want to resolve but that none of them can resolve alone. My role has been as a designer, facilitator, and organizer of these practical social change projects. I have immersed myself in these initiatives, and at the same time have paid attention to what was happening around and inside me.

I have had the privilege of working in this way, alongside my colleagues, with all kinds of teams, on all sorts of challenges, in all parts of the world. We have worked in the United States, to make cities healthier and more livable; in Canada, to accelerate the shift to a low-carbon economy; in Colombia, to create equitable development amid continued polarization; in Guatemala, to implement the peace accords that ended the civil war; across Europe and the Americas, to make food supply chains more sustainable; in Israel, to deal with widening cultural and ideological schisms; in South Africa, to address critical developmental issues in the transition from apartheid; in India, to reduce child malnutrition; in the Philippines, to unblock a political stalemate; and in

Australia, to effect long-delayed reconciliation between aboriginal and nonaboriginal people.

These experiences have given me an up-front view of the dynamics of social change at many levels: individual, group, community, society. I have been a member of tens of diverse teams; working together over months and years; engaging heads, hearts, and hands. I have had the opportunity to participate in much trial and much error and much learning. I have worked side by side with remarkable change agents, social entrepreneurs, and activists, and been able to observe, from both outsider and insider perspectives, what works and what doesn't. Based on these firsthand experiences, I have written this book to share what I have learned with others who are trying to create social change.

Over these twenty years, I have made two discoveries. I reported the first one five years ago in *Solving Tough Problems: An Open Way of Talking, Listening, and Creating New Realities.* In that book I concluded that the key to creating new social realities is to open ourselves up and connect: to our own true selves, to one another, and to our context and what it demands of us.

Five years and many experiences later, I can see that this conclusion was right, but only half right, and dangerously so.

Power and Love picks up where *Solving Tough Problems* left off and reports the second discovery. In order to address our toughest challenges, we must indeed connect, but this is not enough: we must also grow. In other words, we must exercise both love (the drive to unity) and power (the drive to self-realization). If we choose either love or power, we will get stuck in re-creating existing realities, or worse. If we want to create new and better realities—at home, at work, in our communities, in the world—we need to learn how to integrate our love and our power.

Power and Love is both practical and personal. Many researchers—across political science, peace studies, management, neurobiology, sociology, psychology, philosophy, theology—have used a variety of framings and vocabularies to point out the importance of power or love or both. The purpose of this book is not to reiterate or review these specialized theories, but to explore how in general and in practice we can work with power and love to address our toughest challenges. Furthermore, I have not constructed my understanding of these phenomena out of these theories, but instead out of sifting through and trying to make sense of my own most confusing and challenging experiences of social change.

Years ago I was amazed when I read the first pages of the second volume of Lawrence Durrell's novel *The Alexandria Quartet*. Balthazar hands Darley, the narrator, the marked-up manuscript of Darley's first volume: "a paper now seared and starred by a massive interlinear of sentences, paragraphs and question-marks." The second volume then goes on to relate a radically different interpretation of the same events that Darley had described in the first one, and the third and fourth volumes do the same again from two additional perspectives.

Many times during the past twenty years, I have been handed alternative interpretations of my own stories. I am moving along confidently, and then somebody says something that shows me things are not at all the way I think they are. Through such disciplined re-viewing of my own experiences, I have gradually built up my understanding of the dynamics of social change.

The book begins with "Introduction: Beyond War and Peace," which summarizes what I have learned. Chapter 1, "The Two Sides of Power," and Chapter 2, "The Two Sides of Love," describe these two fundamental drives that generate social change. Chapter 3, "The Dilemma of Power and Love," explains why we cannot choose between these drives but must find a way to reconcile them. Chapter 4, "Falling," Chapter 5, "Stumbling," and Chapter 6, "Walking," lay out a progression of three modes of employing power and love—from the most polarized and stuck to the most integrated and fluid—in working collectively to effect social change. In "Conclusion: To Lead Means to Step Forward," I suggest a way to work individually through this same progression, from falling to stumbling to walking, and so become more capable of addressing our toughest challenges.

Introduction:
Beyond War and Peace

*O*UR TWO MOST COMMON ways of trying to address our toughest social challenges are the extreme ones: aggressive war and submissive peace. Neither of these ways works. We can try, using our guns or money or votes, to push through what we want, regardless of what others want—but inevitably the others push back. Or we can try not to push anything on anyone—but that leaves our situation just as it is.

These extreme ways are extremely common, on all scales. One on one, we can be pushy or conflict averse. At work, we can be bossy or "go along to get along." In our communities, we can set things up so that they are the way we want them to be, or we can abdicate. In national affairs, we can make deals to get our way, or we can let others have their way. In international relations—whether the challenge is climate change or trade rules or peace in the Middle East—we can try to impose our solutions on everyone else, or we can negotiate endlessly. These extreme, common ways of trying to address our toughest social challenges usually fail, leaving us stuck and in pain. There are many exceptions to these generalizations about the prevalence of these extreme ways, but the fact that these are exceptions proves the general rule. We need—and many people are working on developing—different, uncommon ways of addressing social challenges: ways beyond these degenerative forms of war and peace.

1

A character in *Rent*, Jonathan Larson's Broadway musical about struggling artists and musicians in New York City, says, "The opposite of war isn't peace, it's creation!"[1] To address our toughest social challenges, we need a way that is neither war nor peace, but collective creation. How can we co-create new social realities?

Two fundamental drives

To co-create new social realities, we have to work with two distinct fundamental forces that are in tension: power and love. This assertion requires an explanation because the words "power" and "love" are defined by so many different people in so many different ways. In this book I use two unusual definitions of power and love suggested by theologian and philosopher Paul Tillich. His definitions are ontological: they deal with what and why power and love are, rather than what they enable or produce. I use these definitions because they ring true with my experience of what in practice is required to address tough challenges at all levels: individual, group, community, society.

Tillich defines *power* as "the drive of everything living to realize itself, with increasing intensity and extensity." So power in this sense is the drive to achieve one's purpose, to get one's job done, to grow. He defines *love* as "the drive towards the unity of the separated."[2] So love in this sense is the drive to reconnect and make whole that which has become or appears fragmented. These two ways of looking at power and love, rather than the more common ideas of oppressive power and romantic love (represented on the cover by the grenade and the rose), are at the core of this book.

Love

Power

OUR FULL WORLD

We cannot address our tough challenges only through driving towards self-realization or only through driving towards unity. We need to do both. Often we assume that all it takes to create something new—whether in business or politics or technology or art—is purposefulness or power. This is because we often assume that the context in which we create is an empty world: an open frontier, a white space, a blank canvas. In general this assumption is incorrect.

Let's look at a historical example. In 1788, British settlers arrived in Australia and encountered the indigenous people who had arrived 40,000 years earlier. This history illustrates not only the courage and entrepreneurialism of people willing to travel across the globe to create a new social reality, but also the human and ecological devastation that this pioneering mind-set can produce. For more than two centuries, the conflict between settlers and aboriginal peoples in Australia was framed in terms of the doctrine of *terra nullius*, a Roman legal term that means "land belonging to no one," or "empty land." It was not until 1992 that the High Court of Australia ruled that the continent had in fact never been *terra nullius*, and that the modern-day settlers had to work out a new way of living together with the aboriginal people.

None of us lives in *terra nullius*. We can pretend that our world is empty, but it is not. Our earth is increasingly full of people and buildings and cars and piles of garbage. Our atmosphere is increasingly full of carbon dioxide. Our society is increasingly full of diverse, strong, competing voices and ideas and cultures. This *fullness* is the fundamental reason why, in order to address our toughest social challenges, we need to employ not only power but also love.

A challenge is tough when it is complex in three ways.[3] A challenge is *dynamically complex* when cause and effect are interdependent and far apart in space and time; such challenges cannot successfully be addressed piece by piece, but only by seeing the system as a whole. A challenge is *socially complex* when the actors involved have different perspectives and interests; such challenges cannot successfully be addressed by experts or authorities, but only with the engagement of the actors themselves. And a challenge is *generatively complex* when its future is fundamentally unfamiliar and undetermined; such challenges cannot successfully be addressed by applying "best practice" solutions from the past, but only by growing new, "next practice" solutions.

The fullness of our world produces this threefold complexity. We can pretend that we are independent and that what we do does not affect others (and what others do does not affect us), but this is not true. We can pretend that everybody sees things the same way, or that our differences can be resolved purely through market or political or legal competition, but this is not true. And we can pretend that we can do things the way we always have, or that we can first figure out and then execute the correct answer, but this is not true.

When we pretend that our world is empty rather than full, and that our challenges are simple rather than complex, we get stuck. If we want to get unstuck, we need to acknowledge our interdependence, cooperate, and feel our way forward. We need therefore to employ not only our power but also our love. If this sounds easy, it is not. It is difficult and dangerous.

what shall we do?

Two pitfalls

Power and love are difficult to work with because each of them has two sides. Power has a generative side and a degenerative side, and—less obviously—love also has a generative side and a degenerative side. Feminist scholar Paola Melchiori pointed out to me that we can see these two sets of two sides if we look at historically constructed gender roles. The father, embodying masculine power, goes out to work, to do his job. The generative side of his power is that he can create something valuable in the world. The degenerative side of his power is that he can become so focused on his work that he denies his connection to his colleagues and family, and so becomes a robot or a tyrant.

The mother, by contrast, embodying feminine love, stays at home to raise the children. The generative side of her love is that she gives life, literally to her child and figuratively to her whole family. The degenerative side of her love is that she can become so identified with and embracing of her child and family that she denies their and especially her own need for self-realization, and so stunts their and her own growth.[4]

Love is what makes power generative instead of degenerative. Power is what makes love generative instead of degenerative. Power and love are therefore exactly complementary. In order for each to achieve its full potential, it needs the other. Just as the *terra nullius* perspective of focusing only on power is an error, so too is the pop perspective that "all you need is love."

Psychologist Rollo May, a friend of Paul Tillich, warned of the dangers of disconnecting power (which he referred to as "will") from love. "Love and will," he wrote, "are interdependent and belong together. Both are conjunctive processes of being— a reaching out to influence others, molding, forming, creating the consciousness of the other. But this is only possible, in an inner sense, if one opens oneself at the same time to the influence of the other. Will without love becomes manipulation and love without will becomes sentimental. The bottom then drops out of the conjunctive emotions and processes."[5] May's conjunctive processes also operate on a social level, and we can effect nonviolent social change only if we can engage both our power and our love.

One of the greatest practitioners of nonviolent social change, Martin Luther King Jr., was both a practical activist and a spiritual leader. He demonstrated a way of addressing tough social challenges that went beyond aggressive war and submissive peace, thereby contributing to the creation of new social realities in the United States and around the world. In his last presidential speech to the Southern Christian Leadership Conference, King— drawing on his doctoral studies of Tillich's work—emphasized the essential complementarity between power and love.[6] "Power without love is reckless and abusive," King said, "and love without power is sentimental and anemic."[7]

My own experience of the past twenty years entirely bears out King's analysis. Power without love *is* reckless and abusive. If those of us engaged in social change act to realize ourselves without recognizing that we and others are interdependent, the result will at best be insensitive and at worst, oppressive or even genocidal. And love without power *is* sentimental and anemic. If we recognize our interdependence and act to unify with others, but do so in a way that hobbles our own or others' growth, the result will at best be ineffectual and at worst, deceitfully reinforcing of the status quo.

Power without love produces scorched-earth war that destroys everything we hold dear. Love without power produces lifeless peace that leaves us stuck in place. Both of these are terrible outcomes. We need to find a better way.

In his speech, King went on to say, "This collision of immoral power with powerless morality constitutes the major crisis of our time."[8] This collision continues because our polarization of power and love continues. In our societies and communities and organizations, and within each of us, we usually find a "power camp," which pays attention to interests and differences, and a "love camp," which pays attention to connections and commonalities. The collision between these two camps—in the worlds of business, politics, and social change, among others—impedes our ability to make progress on our toughest social challenges.

AN IMPERATIVE

Power and love stand at right angles and delineate the space of social change. If we want to get unstuck and to move around this space—if we want to address our toughest challenges—we must understand and work with both of these drives.

Rather than a choice to be made one way or another, power and love constitute a permanent dilemma that must be reconciled continuously and creatively. This reconciliation is easy in theory but hard in practice. Carl Jung doubted whether it was even possible for these two drives to coexist in the same person: "Where love reigns, there is no will to power; and where the will power is paramount, love is lacking. The one is but the shadow of the other."[9] His student Robert Johnson said, "Probably the most troublesome pair of opposites that we can try to reconcile is love and power. Our modern world is torn to shreds by this dichotomy, and one finds many more failures than successes in the attempt to reconcile them."[10]

I have seen many examples of reckless and abusive power without love, and many examples of sentimental and anemic love without power. I have seen far fewer examples of power with love. Too few of us are capable of employing power with love. More of us need to learn.

If we are to succeed in co-creating new social realities, we cannot choose between power and love. We must choose both. This book explores how.

1
The Two Sides of Power

O EXPLAIN WHERE I have arrived in my under
standing of power and love and social change,
I have to explain how I started.

I grew up in Montreal and studied physics at McGill University. In the summer of 1981, as I was finishing my undergraduate degree, I attended a meeting of the Pugwash Conference on Science and World Affairs in Banff, Alberta, where I heard a speech about the crucial energy and environmental challenges arising out of the increasing complexity and fullness—of people and ideas and things—of the world. I decided to shift my studies from physical to social sciences, and I went on to do a graduate degree in economics and public policy at the University of California at Berkeley. After graduation, I worked at a variety of research institutions in North America, Europe, and Asia, and then in the corporate planning department of Pacific Gas and Electric Company in San Francisco.

My father had taught me the value of industriousness—of doing my job well, whatever that job was—and of self-determination and self-improvement. His favorite story was of Henry David Thoreau, who had lived in the woods at Walden Pond and after two years had come out with his axe sharper than when he had gone in.

I was young and ambitious and keen to make my mark on the world.

Generative power

In 1988, when I was twenty-seven years old, I moved from San Francisco to London to take a job in the global strategy department of the energy company Royal Dutch Shell. What I loved most about working for Shell was the power. I enjoyed getting the diplomatic memos: "The government of Côte d'Ivoire has reiterated their request that we desist from referring to them as the Ivory Coast." I once got a mistaken phone call asking me where a $300 million payment for a fuel oil delivery should be deposited. I liked Shell's practical role in providing the world with energy: the company invested hundreds of millions of dollars a year in research and development, drilled for oil thousands of feet underwater, and produced fuels by heating oil sands and cooling natural gas. I reveled in being a small cog in this big and important machine.

I was at Shell at the height of capitalist confidence. The Berlin Wall had just fallen, the Internet boom was starting, Francis Fukuyama had published "The End of History," Tom Wolfe was writing about Manhattan financiers as "Masters of the Universe," and Margaret Thatcher was pronouncing that "There Is No Alternative" to the Anglo-American free enterprise model. The dominant cultural meme was that in all spheres—economic, political, social, legal, international, intellectual—a contest among competing powers produced the best outcome.[1] From my office in a London skyscraper, it seemed to me that if everybody just did their job and pushed forward their part—engaged in civilized, manly jostling—the whole would grow and prosper.

My experience at Shell, and elsewhere in the world of business, was of an almost single-minded emphasis on the pragmatic use of power—the kind of power that a former physics student could recognize. It seemed to me that businesspeople understood power the same way Martin Luther King Jr. did: "Power properly understood is nothing but the ability to achieve purpose."[2] Their actions seemed to accord with Paul Tillich's explanation of power's generative root: "the drive of everything living to realize itself, with increasing intensity and extensity." This drive can be seen in the force of a growing seed: the force that "guerrilla gardeners" employ to turn vacant urban lots into parks, when they surreptitiously plant seeds that break through the concrete.

At Shell I could see how my own drive for self-realization, along with that of my colleagues, produced furiously competitive intellectual creativity and growth. The head of our department, Arie de Geus, wrote a book called *The Living Company*. This helped me also see how the company's living drive for self-realization, along with that of other companies, produced furiously competitive commercial creativity and growth.[3]

In all of this I saw the generative aspect of power: the universal drive to "get one's job done." Power expresses our purposefulness, wholeness, and agency. Although power is the drive to realize one's self, the effect of power goes beyond one's self. Power is how we make a difference in the world; it is the means by which new social realities are created. Without power, nothing new grows.

At Shell I was head of the strategy group that constructed scenarios—plausible alternative stories—of social-political-environmental contexts in which the company might find itself. In 1991, Pieter le Roux, a professor at the left-wing University of the Western Cape in South Africa, contacted me because he wanted to use the Shell methodology to help a group of South African opposition leaders develop a strategy for effecting the transition away from apartheid. Nelson Mandela had just been released from twenty-seven years in prison, and the negotiations between the opposition and the white minority government had started in earnest. Le Roux's project sounded interesting and worthwhile to me, and my Shell bosses were happy, after years of being vilified for not having divested from South Africa, for the opportunity to rebuild the company's relationships with the opposition. So in September 1991, I traveled to Cape Town to facilitate the first workshop of what became known as the Mont Fleur Scenario Exercise.[4]

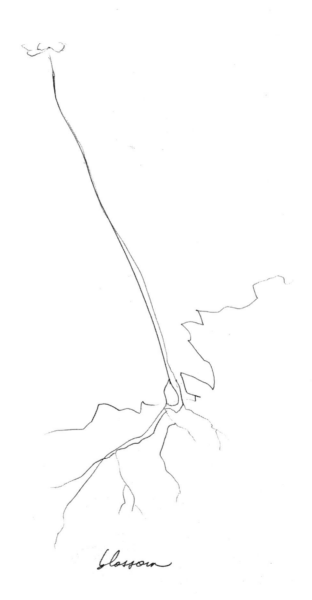

blossom

What I found exhilarating in meeting these leaders—from political parties, trade unions, community organizations, universities, and companies—was their powerful purposefulness. Every one of them was committed to addressing, from their particular idiological and institutional base, South Africa's tough challenges, and they had already realized that they could be successful only if they worked together. White businessman Johann Liebenberg later remembered, with surprise and pleasure, his conversations with the black leaders who had hitherto been his adversaries: "This was new to me, especially how open-minded they were. These were not people who simply said: 'Look, this is how it is going to be when we take over one day.' They were prepared to say: 'Hey, how *would* it be? Let's discuss it.'"[5] I felt excited to play a part in this important social change process.

What I saw in these workshops, and through the window they provided me onto the dynamics of South Africa's extraordinary transition, changed my understanding of what was possible in the world. I saw that a team of leaders from across a social system could, even in the most complex, conflictual, and challenging of contexts, exercise their power collectively to change that system for the better. I was inspired by what I was learning about this generative power.

What I saw also changed my understanding of what was possible for me. I saw that I had a job to do—a way of making a difference in the world—in supporting such teams. In 1993, I resigned from Shell and moved to South Africa. Since then I have been doing this kind of work there and elsewhere.

DEGENERATIVE POWER

How do we come to notice something that we are not noticing? I was once working in my office, and my sunglasses were in my shirt pocket. I went into a dark closet and leaned over to pick up some supplies near the floor, when I heard a sound that I couldn't place. As I went out, I unconsciously filed away that anomalous event—the unexplained sound—and went back to what I was doing. Later I saw that I had misplaced my sunglasses and began looking all around for them. Then I remembered the unexplained sound and realized it had been the sound of my sunglasses falling out of my pocket onto the closet floor.

During the first years after I left Shell and started working as a facilitator of social change teams, I kept hearing sounds of a second kind of power that I didn't know how to interpret. My first interpretation of what had happened at Mont Fleur— the interpretation that I was working from—was that the team had decided that their power, their drive to realize themselves as individuals and as a nation, could more effectively be exercised working with rather than against one another. They had used four bird images to summarize their shared understanding of the different ways the future of the nation might unfold: an "Ostrich" scenario of white denial, a "Lame Duck" scenario of an overconstrained new black government, an "Icarus" scenario of the new government flying too high too fast, and a "Flamingos" scenario of rising slowly together. But when Pallo Jordan, one of the intellectual leaders of the African National Congress, heard these scenarios presented at a party meeting, he thought they were ridiculously naïve about the essentially violent dynamics of power in the South African context. "What is all this about ducks and flamingos?" he asked incredulously. "The only birds that matter here are hawks and sparrows!"

It is not surprising that Jordan and I had different perspectives on power. I came from a peaceful and unfettered background, and I had encountered South Africa for the first time in 1991, one year after the hopeful transitional negotiations had started and several years after the hopeless, violent clashes between the government and the opposition in the 1970s and 1980s. Jordan is black, which in apartheid South Africa means he grew up as a second-class person. He had spent decades in exile working for the African National Congress and had only just returned to the country to engage directly in these tough negotiations. Power looks different to people who have to struggle for it.

Now I realized what I had been hearing: power has two sides. The generative side of power is the *power-to* that Paul Tillich refers to as the drive to self-realization. The degenerative, shadow side is *power-over*—the stealing or suppression of the self-realization of another. Tillich recognizes both sides: "Power actualizes itself through force and compulsion. But power is neither the one nor the other. It is being, actualizing itself over non-being. It uses and abuses compulsion in order to overcome this threat. It uses and abuses force in order to actualize itself. But it is neither the one nor the other."[6] Power-over abuses force and compulsion to suppress or oppress or dominate another.

Like Pallo Jordan, my wife Dorothy is black and grew up in South Africa and was involved for years in the anti-apartheid struggle. When later we visited Guatemala together, she noticed something that I didn't. The position of aboriginal people there reminded her of blacks in South Africa: they were treated as if they were invisible. Not to see another person, or to see her or him as a nonperson, is the extreme manifestation of power-over.

The most common understanding of power is as power-over. When Stephen Lukes, a professor of politics and sociology at New York University, wrote his classic 1974 book *Power: A Radical View*, he equated power with domination. But thirty years later, in the second edition, Lukes revised his view: "It was a mistake to define power by saying that 'A exercises power over B when A affects B in a manner contrary to B's interests.' Power as domination is only one species of power."[7] Power-over is a subset of power-to.

Degenerative power-over arises out of generative power-to. When I am exercising my power-to and I feel myself bumping up against you exercising yours, and if in this conflict I have the capacity to prevail over you, then I can easily turn to exercising power over you. My drive to realize myself slips easily into valuing my self-realization above yours, and then into believing arrogantly that I am more deserving of self-realization, and then into advancing my self-realization even if it impedes yours.

Many whites in South Africa valued their self-realization above that of others, and they deployed an ideology—apartheid—to justify their behavior. We can see analogous dynamics across races or ethnic groups or classes or genders in every society. Thus, the seductively beautiful face of power-to morphs, as in a horror movie, into the viciously terrible face of power-over.

Once I had seen the two sides of power starkly in South Africa, I could recognize them more easily elsewhere. After I left Shell, I consulted to several companies and business associations in Houston, Texas. I found the business culture of Houston unusual and fascinating. The businesspeople there were unconstrained in their enthusiasm for independent, unregulated, entrepreneurial power-to. The can-do property developers I met owned private companies with names like "John Smith Interests," which I understood to represent an unabashed celebration of the advancing of an individual's own interests and power.

These same businesspeople were also enthusiastic in their support for voluntary philanthropy and civic engagement. They were more aware than people I had met elsewhere of their role in the evolution of their social reality. Houston had grown from being the twenty-first largest city in the United States in 1940 to fourth largest in 1990. It had become what it was not by accident, but as the result of the intentional decisions made by people such as themselves, and they felt a responsibility to continue this public work. The ideology of Houston businesspeople promoted individual self-realization in alignment with collective self-realization.

In this community, the very epitome of power-to was Ken Lay, the founder and chairman of Enron, the $100 billion natural gas, electricity, and telecommunications company. Enron had been named "America's Most Innovative Company" by *Fortune* magazine six years in a row, and Lay was admired as an entrepreneurial genius. At Shell, young staff who considered themselves to be sophisticated strategists were in awe of Enron's deal making. The company was one of Houston's biggest employers and charitable donors, and it had sponsored a popular new downtown stadium. When Lay visited our Houston workshops, the other business leaders treated him like a god. Lay symbolized the virtues of the free marketeer whose unfettered power–to produced both private wealth and public good.

In 2001, I chaired a Business Leaders' Dialogue at the Aspen Institute in Colorado. Among the participants, who included international corporate, government, trade union, and nonprofit leaders, Lay was the star whom everyone wanted to meet. By this time, stories about Enron's malfeasance were beginning to circulate. The most prominent accusation against Enron was that it had illegally manipulated California's electricity market, and California attorney general Bill Lockyer was calling for Lay to be prosecuted.

Lay's way of participating in our meeting was striking. He moved in and out of the sessions, which we had all agreed not to do and which no one else did. He seemed to hold himself apart from or above the group. He was the only dissenter from the group's conclusion that corporate social responsibility should be enforced rather than left voluntary. The only time he participated passionately was when, with righteous indignation, he told the story about Lockyer having threatened him by saying, "I would love to personally escort Lay to an 8-by-10 cell that he could share with a tattooed dude who says, 'Hi, my name is Spike, honey.'"[8]

During these sessions, only one other participant, a trade unionist, ever challenged Lay. Everyone else conspicuously deferred to him. I thought that if Lay was so powerful and wealthy, he deserved to be looked up to, and also that if I was polite to him, I might benefit from his largesse.

One year after the Aspen Institute meeting, Enron declared bankruptcy, and five years after, Lay was found guilty of ten charges of fraud and conspiracy. The company's collapse wiped out more than $60 billion in shareholder investment and 6,000 employee jobs, and led to the dissolution of Arthur Andersen, its auditor.

Exercising creative, entrepreneurial, profitable power-to is not hard if you pretend, and are allowed to pretend, that you live in an unregulated *terra nullius*. But Lay and his Enron colleagues did not live in such an empty world, and in defrauding millions of people, they severely undermined those people's power-to. Lay's emphatic rejection of rules that govern the collective, as manifested in his disinterest (enabled by our deference) in the small matter of our meeting's ground rules and the larger matter of U.S. law, illustrated his disconnected, degenerative power-over.

The irresponsible power-over exercised by Enron executives foreshadowed the global financial collapse of 2008. Business journalist Mark Haines was flummoxed when the crisis broke: "We assume that the individual pursuing his or her own best interest will result in the maximum benefit for society as a whole—and that certainly has to be questioned now."[9] The understanding that I had imbibed in London twenty years earlier—that a system driven by the power-to of the parts would produce a beneficial result for the whole—was tragically incomplete and inadequate. Before this became apparent, however, I was to have other experiences that led me to my current understanding of degenerative power.

those hornets feed on self & other

When, after Mont Fleur, I had started working on different tough challenges in different countries—power-over manifesting in inequity and inequality—I carried with me a certain confidence that I came from a country, Canada, that had successfully overcome its own such challenges. So in 2003 I was taken aback to find myself in a conference room at the Department of Justice in Ottawa, Ontario, listening to a group of leaders of government, business, and aboriginal (Native or First Nations) organizations talk about their encounters with the realities of aboriginal people in Canada.

As we went around the table and heard each person's story—of extraordinarily high levels of poverty, addiction, and suicide; decades of abuse by "well-intentioned" governments and churches; conflicts over the extraction of oil and other natural resources; thousands of stuck land and treaty disputes—it became obvious to me that I did *not* come from a country that had successfully overcome such challenges. My colleague Ursula Versteegen says that our most important learnings come not simply when we see the world anew, but specifically when we see ourselves—and our role in creating the world—anew.[10] On that day I saw that I was part of a society that was exercising a terrible power-over.

One aspect of this Canadian situation was the widely held mental model that aboriginal people needed to "be developed." This model had been institutionalized in, among other practices, a policy of aggressive assimilation that since the 1850s had taken children away from their parents to be educated in church- and state-run residential schools. One of the founders of residential schooling in North America characterized his approach as "kill the Indian and save the man."[11] Residential schooling created a legacy of physical, emotional, sexual, and cultural abuse. By the time the last residential school in Canada closed in 1998, this power over aboriginal people had been replicated for generations.

After this meeting in Ottawa, I and a few colleagues began working with a team of national government and aboriginal leaders to try out a new way to unstick this stuck situation. We chose as our entry point the extraordinarily high rate of suicide among aboriginal youth: five times the Canadian average. But after four years of on-and-off efforts, we had hardly moved forward at all. We kept running into roadblocks, large and small. At one point we were frustrated in trying to communicate with the staff of an aboriginal-run conference center. I complained about this to my friend, activist Michel Gelobter, and he chided me: "Why are you surprised that oppressed communities exhibit serious dysfunctions? These dysfunctions have to be recognized and dealt with; they reinforce and maintain oppression by diminishing the capacity of these communities to heal." The degenerative impacts of power-over are resolutely persistent.

I also noticed that within our microcosmic project team, we succeeded in re-creating the stuck relationships that characterized the macrocosm we were trying to change. The government leaders wanted to remain in control and to "fix" the aboriginal problem. The aboriginal leaders didn't want to be controlled or fixed or developed by anyone. And those of us who were consultants dispassionately kept ourselves apart from and above the situation. We all had our own different roles and powers and trajectories of self-realization, which never really moved and never really met. So we made no progress on the challenge that we had set out to address. (Only later, when these roles and power relations were forcefully restructured and ownership of the project was taken over by a local aboriginal community, did the initiative begin to move forward.)

In Canada, as in South Africa and Houston, I had been able to recognize the sound of power-to more easily than the sound of power-over because the former resonated more strongly with my own privileged experience. Then in 2004 I got a taste of the experience of the underside of power-over. My London partner Zaid Hassan and I were invited to facilitate a workshop in Michigan for a group of U.S. minority activists who were rethinking their strategy for achieving racial equity in light of the just-issued Supreme Court decision that sharply limited affirmative action.

I was unsettled even before the meeting started. Zaid is Muslim and I am Jewish, and on the plane ride he had shown me an article in an activist magazine that pointed out how many of the U.S. neoconservatives are Jewish. He also showed me a letter to the editor that he had written, in which he acknowledged how contentious this assertion was but defended it as informative and fair. We started into a tense discussion, a fractal of the larger Muslim-Jewish conflict, but then cut short our argument to get ready for the workshop.

With this unresolved tension between Zaid and me, the workshop started awkwardly and got worse. The participants were feeling beaten down by the regression in civil rights in the United States and discouraged about the poor results their existing strategies were producing. They didn't think my leadership of the meeting, with my white and foreign colleagues, was legitimate, and they were unhappy with the process we were using. Harsh power struggles swirled around and within the room. Eventually it became obvious that I wasn't wanted in the workshop at all, and so, feeling humiliated, I gave up. I left the group to lead itself and went back to my room.

That night I had a terrifying dream. A gang was harassing me mercilessly—crowding and shoving and hitting me—and I couldn't escape. Eventually I became so hopeless and despairing that I pulled the pin out of a hand grenade and blew myself up with all of them: I became a suicide bomber. Through this dream I experienced the terrible, debilitating feeling of being on the receiving end of power-over.

By 2008, my understanding of the dynamics of power and love was taking shape through such experiences and reflections. Then I had another encounter with aboriginal issues, this time in Australia. I was invited to Melbourne by an Australian aboriginal leader named Patrick Dodson. He is well known for his decades of varied struggles—mobilizations, negotiations, invocations, lawsuits—to address the challenges faced by his people, and specifically for his efforts to achieve reconciliation between aboriginal and nonaboriginal Australians.[12] He knows how hard it is to move forward on these challenges and wasn't surprised by the lack of progress of the effort in Canada in which I had been involved.

Dodson wanted me to contribute to a meeting that he was convening with John Sanderson, the former chief of the Australian Army. They were trying to construct a new set of agreements (including constitutional amendments) that would, more than 220 years after the arrival of the settlers and 15 years after the High Court verdict that overruled *terra nullius*, put the relationship between these two peoples on an equal footing.

The evening before our meetings were to start, I walked by an outdoor cinema and found myself watching two documentaries. The first was *The White Planet*, a film about arctic wildlife and the dangers it faces from global warming.[13] The second was *Kanyini*, about an Australian aboriginal leader named Bob Randall, a member of the "Stolen Generation" who as a child had (like many Canadian children) been taken away from his family by the government.[14] In *Kanyini*, Randall argues that the crisis in aboriginal society originated in their having been dispossessed and estranged from the four aspects of life that are essential to survival: their belief system or law, their land or country, their spirituality, and their families. "The purpose of life is to be part of everything that is," he says in the film. "You take away my *kanyini*, my interconnectedness, and I'm nothing. I'm dead."

I was struck that Randall's yearning was the same as Paul Tillich's love: "the drive towards the unity of the separated."

In the juxtaposition of these two films, I could now see what happens when we employ our power without love. Our destruction of aboriginal societies worldwide and our headlong rush towards the destruction of the ecosystems on which all our societies depend arise from our disconnection from one another and from the earth. Environmentalist Julia Butterfly Hill made the same point in describing her unlikely partnership with social activist Van Jones: "I brought the piece that we are not separate from the planet. His piece was that we need to uplift everyone. We were committed to seeing how those pieces fit together. We could see underneath all of it was the idea of disposability: the idea that you've got disposable people, a disposable planet."[15] If we push away or abandon our sense of connection with others— our acknowledgment, our sensitivity, our love—there is no limit to the sadness, terror, and pain that our unchecked power can produce.

We can recognize this degenerative phenomenon of power without love because, in so many contexts and at so many scales, power dominates love. We see this in our homes, organizations, communities, nations, and in international affairs. Patrick Dodson told me a story about Michael Long, a popular Australian aboriginal sportsman who had walked from Melbourne to Canberra to draw attention to the desperate situation of his people. Long met with Prime Minister John Howard and asked him the anguished question: "Where is the love for my people?" We all feel the anguish that results from the deficit of love.

LOVE IS WHAT MAKES POWER GENERATIVE

Based on these experiences, then, here is how I understand the nature of power and its relationship to love. Power has two sides, one generative and the other degenerative. Our power is generative and amplifying when we realize ourselves while loving and uniting with others. Our power is degenerative and constraining—reckless and abusive, or worse—when we overlook or deny or cut off our love and unity.

opening

2

The Two Sides of Love

HE MONT FLEUR PROJECT showed me a doorway into a new world. I was drawn to what I could see, through the project, of the way South Africans were bridging their differences and together exercising generative power. I was also drawn to the project coordinator, Dorothy Boesak. In 1993, I walked through this doorway: I resigned from Shell, moved from London to Cape Town, started working full time on multi-stakeholder social change projects, married Dorothy, and became the stepfather of her four teenage children. This new world taught me a lot about love.

GENERATIVE LOVE

I fell in love with Dorothy—but this book is not about romantic love. It is about something else that I experienced in meeting her. I noticed that Dorothy had a way of relating with other people that was different from mine. Compared to me, she was more considerate and generous in her dealings with family, neighbors, even strangers. She was more focused on what was needed of her and less on what she needed. Dorothy was an accomplished and respected professional and community leader, but she was less focused on realizing herself than I was. She seemed to be driven by something else. I sensed there was something here for me to learn.

Dorothy and I had different approaches to parenting. When we were first married and would disagree about the kids, the poles of our disagreement were always the same. I thought they needed to be pushed to stand on their own two feet: to study, to work, to move out of the house—and to her this seemed callous. Dorothy also wanted to help the kids grow, but she thought they needed to be held in the bosom of the family: to be looked after, nurtured, sheltered—and to me this seemed indulgent.

After Mont Fleur, Dorothy started her own business helping people in her community with their savings and investments, and she wasn't much interested in being involved in my consulting work. But we did work together once, on a strategy workshop for the Synod of Anglican Bishops. Dorothy chose to sit in the meeting room and listen, and during the breaks she talked with the bishops. When we read the participants' daily feedback, I was struck that they appreciated what both of us had done and saw our two roles as making up an integral whole. They experienced her quiet connectedness to be as valuable as my vocal directiveness.

I have come to see these complementarities between my and Dorothy's orientations and behaviors as expressing the complementary drives of power and love. Paul Tillich's power as the drive towards self-realization is manifested in a focus on self-expression and self-growth. Love as the drive to unite the separated is manifested in a focus on relationship and connection. Dorothy and I both had both drives, but in each of us a different one was dominant.

After I moved to South Africa, I looked for a way to continue with the vocation that I had discovered at Mont Fleur. I ended up cofounding an international consulting firm called Generon with two men twenty-five years my senior: Bill O'Brien and Joseph Jaworski. They also taught me a lot about love.

Bill O'Brien had been the president of Hanover Insurance Company for twelve years, during which time the company had gone from the bottom to the top of the U.S. property and liability insurance industry. Bill had an innovative management philosophy that inspired Peter Senge of the Massachusetts Institute of Technology in his founding of the Society for Organizational Learning and his writing of *The Fifth Discipline*.[1] Peter says about Bill: "There is no business person from whom I have learned more."[2]

When I became the managing partner of Generon, Bill, seeing that I was ill prepared, took it upon himself to mentor me. I was surprised and touched by this relationship because it was obvious that Bill's primary interest was in helping me realize myself. He paid particular attention to the process of maturation. He thought the self-interested ambition—the will to power—that is healthy in a twenty-year-old is no longer healthy in a sixty-year-old. He told me that the philosopher Pierre Teilhard de Chardin realized he was becoming mature when he could read a newspaper story that had a favorable impact on society and a negative impact on himself, and be happy.

Bill's management philosophy included a pragmatic practice of love, which he described this way:

> In our Western world, the word "love" has deep connotations we do not normally associate with business—romance, for example, or that special feeling among family members or close friends. But I am not talking about these kinds of relationships. By "love," I mean a predisposition toward helping another person to become complete: to develop to their full potential. Love is not something that suddenly strikes us—it is an act of the will. By "an act of will," I mean that you do not have to like someone to love him or her. Love is an intentional disposition toward another person.[3]

Humberto Maturana, a Chilean cognitive biologist who also worked with Peter Senge at the Society for Organizational Learning, offers a similar definition: "Love is the domain of those relational behaviors through which another (a person, being, or thing) arises as a legitimate other in coexistence with oneself."[4] And Jungian Robert Johnson writes "Love is the one power that awakens the ego to the existence of something outside itself."[5] All of these definitions, from the worlds of management, biology, and psychology, are congruent with Paul Tillich's from theology. Love is the other-acknowledging, other-respecting, other-helping drive that reunites the separated.

———

In 1998, I started working on a project in Guatemala, inspired by Mont Fleur, to support the implementation of the peace accords that two years earlier had ended that country's brutal thirty-six-year civil war. Visión Guatemala brought together leaders of many of the factions that had been involved, in one way or another, in this violent conflict: cabinet ministers, former army and guerrilla officers, businessmen, journalists, young people, aboriginal people. This team worked together over two years and contributed to the creation of a new national reality.[6]

A pivotal event in the project occurred on the second evening of the team's first workshop. The team was sitting in a circle, telling stories about their experiences of the previous years. A man named Ronalth Ochaeta, a human rights worker for the Catholic Church, told about the time he went to an aboriginal village to witness the exhumation of a mass grave from one of the war's many massacres. When the earth was removed, he noticed a number of small bones and asked the forensics team if people had their bones broken during the massacre. They replied that, no, the grave contained the corpses of pregnant women, and the small bones were those of their fetuses.

a radical meeting

When Ochaeta finished telling his story, the team was completely silent. I had never experienced a silence like this, and I was struck dumb. The silence lasted a long time; to me it seemed like five minutes. Then it ended and we continued with our work.

This episode made a deep impact on the team and on me. When members of the team were interviewed two years later for a project history, many of them traced their collective strength, which enabled them to do the important work they went on to do, to the insight and connection manifested in those minutes of silence. One of them said, "After listening to Ochaeta's story, I understood and felt in my heart all that had happened. And there was a feeling that we must struggle to prevent this from happening again." Another said, "In giving his testimony, Ochaeta was sincere, calm, and serene, without a trace of hate in his voice. This gave way to the moment of silence that, I would say, lasted at least one minute. It was horrible! It was a very moving experience for all of us. If you ask any of us, we would say that this moment was like a large communion."[7]

A moment of team communion is a moment of a team being one body. This was the motive force of Visión Guatemala: a loving drive towards the unity of the separated. The civil war had torn Guatemalan society apart, and the project brought together the leaders of these estranged parts to connect with one another and thereby begin to reconnect the society as a whole. All of the turning points in the project were moments when the team saw the reality of Guatemala through each other's eyes and saw each other, not as faceless enemies or as primitive nonpersons, but as brothers and sisters, part of one whole.

Humberto Maturana says that love is the only emotion that expands intelligence.[8] The love experienced by the members of Visión Guatemala expanded their intelligence and increased their capacity to contribute to the healing and growth of their country.

Lars Franklin, the United Nations representative in Guatemala, said that Visión Guatemala could best be understood by looking at the many seeds it planted and nurtured. These included influencing the platforms of three political parties; participating in the vital commissions on Historical Clarification, the Peace Accords, and a Fiscal Pact; and contributing to a constitutional amendment campaign, a national antipoverty program, many municipal development strategies, and the reform of both primary school and university curricula. Project coordinator Elena Díez also supported team members in launching several influential successor dialogue groups among stakeholders in the education system, among leftist leaders, among indigenous leaders, and among politicians from twenty parties.

The story of the five minutes of silence in Visión Guatemala became the crowning chapter in my book *Solving Tough Problems*. It epitomized my understanding of the centrality of love—of opening up and connecting—to addressing tough social challenges. I could see that almost all of the leaders I was working with around the world had stepped forward to engage in these collective challenge-addressing processes because they saw themselves as part of unhealthy and unwhole systems that they felt a responsibility to contribute to repairing. Their drive towards unity contributed not only to healing these systems, but also to healing themselves and me.

When I met Dorothy and started doing this social change work, my power drive was stronger than my love drive. Maybe this was because I had grown up the eldest of three sons of an assertive father, or maybe it was my own particular, lopsided maturing path. Now I was discovering, at home and at work, that I also had a capacity for love. A colleague who watched me facilitate told me that I had a gift for weaving people's contributions together. This made me think of my mother, who had focused her energies on raising us lovingly and, after we were grown, took up textile weaving; her particular interest was in harmoniously combining different colors and textures. Now, as I was completing myself, I was starting to pick up some of her capacities.[9]

One of my Guatemalan colleagues had been taught by the Jesuits that having a gift should be treated not as a virtue but as a responsibility. After all, because it is given to you, a gift is not something for which you can take credit.[10] I thought that I had a responsibility to use my gift for weaving.

My partner Joseph Jaworski helped me make sense of what I was observing in Guatemala and in myself. Joseph had been a trial lawyer and businessman. His father was Watergate Special Prosecutor Leon Jaworski, and in conversations with his father, Joseph had seen an unwholeness in American public leadership that he was moved to contribute to repairing. In 1980, Joseph founded the American Leadership Forum, which brought diverse groups of leaders in various U.S. cities to learn and act together. In 1990, he was recruited into Shell to lead the scenario team, and this is how he and I started working together.

For Joseph, relationships are primary. In his experiences in packed courtrooms, in the devastated aftermath of a tornado, at a racetrack, and in one-on-one meetings, he has felt the separation between himself and others disappear. In 1980, he spoke with quantum physicist and dialogue practitioner David Bohm, who told him, "The most important thing going forward is to break the boundaries between people, so we can operate as a single intelligence. This is the natural state of the human world, separation without separateness."[11]

Joseph has spent years working purposefully to understand and explain these experiences, and he wrote about them in *Synchronicity: The Inner Path of Leadership*. In the foreword, Peter Senge wrote, "Because of our obsession with how leaders behave, we forget that in its essence, leadership is about learning how to shape the future. Leadership is about creating new realities."[12] Joseph believes that leaders trying to create new realities require the capacity to unite the separated. The distinctive dimension of Generon's consulting work, with both corporate and multi-stakeholder leadership teams, was supporting the development of this pragmatic capacity for love.

While we were doing this consulting, we were also building up an underlying body of theory and practice. Joseph under-took a research project with Otto Scharmer of the Massachu-setts Institute of Technology, which included interviews with 150 leading scientists, artists, social entrepreneurs, and business-people around the world about their experiences with effecting profound innovation and change. One of the people they inter-viewed was Brian Arthur, an economist at the Santa Fe Institute, who had done pioneering work in complexity science. Arthur helped them crystallize the pattern they were hearing in their interviews: that profound innovation includes three movements, which can be represented in the shape of a U. The first move-ment, descending the left side of the U, they called "sensing": developing a felt sense of the current reality of the system that we are trying to understand and change. The second movement, at the bottom of the U, they called "presencing": tapping into—becoming fully present to—a deeper knowing about our role in the system and what is needed of us. The third movement, ascending the right side of the U, they called "realizing": acting from this place of deeper knowing to bring forth a new reality.

Otto Scharmer and Joseph Jaworski proposed the *U-Process* as a general theory for understanding and implementing the cre-ation of new realities. They wrote up their findings, with Peter Senge and Betty Sue Flowers, in *Presence: Human Purpose and the Field of the Future*, and later Otto Scharmer published a fuller exposition in *Theory U: Leading from the Future as It Emerges*.[13]

One radical aspect of this U-Process is its emphasis on uniting the creative leader with other stakeholders, with the larger context, and with his or her own higher self. I recognized in this description of the three movements of individual innovation the process of collective innovation that I had seen in Guatemala and elsewhere. The many days that the Visión Guatemala team spent developing a collective map of their situation—sharing experiences and perspectives among themselves; interacting with resource persons; going on field trips; synthesizing their understanding into a set of scenarios—constituted their "co-sensing." In the course of uncovering their reality, and especially of the part that each of them played in its enactment and hence what was needed of them, the team was "co-presencing." This occurred many times, but for the first time and most dramatically in the open-hearted silence that followed Ronalth Ochaeta's story. Finally, the extended series of actions that the team took over the years that followed to effect change in Guatemala was their "co-realizing."

By 2001, we in Generon were confident that our practice and theory for co-creating new social realities were mature enough for us to take our work to the next level. In partnership with the Society for Organizational Learning, we set up a nonprofit "Global Leadership Initiative" and articulated our intention to apply our U-Process in large-scale multi-stakeholder "change labs." We proposed to contribute to solving ten complex and vital global social problems and thereby demonstrate that it is possible with love to change history. "Our goal," we wrote, "is nothing less than to generate a 'tipping point' in humanity's ability to address its most critical global challenges."

In the years that followed, we invested everything we had in this initiative. We formed a team of ten persons, negotiated partnerships with several big companies and nonprofits, raised millions of dollars, and developed a series of audacious projects addressing challenges related to sustainable food, wilderness protection, HIV/AIDS, water shortages, child malnutrition, and aboriginal youth.

Things did not, however, turn out quite the way we planned.

DEGENERATIVE LOVE

In 2005, I gave a speech in Halifax about our vision for the Global Leadership Initiative and my understanding of how to effect social change. In the question-and-answer period that followed, a Palestinian activist named Zoughbi Zoughbi asked me a question that I should have recognized as a hint, even a warning. "Adam," he said, "the aspect of this systemic change work that I don't hear you talking about is power. How do you deal with power?" I heard his point but—enamored as I was with love—didn't think what he was saying was important. I answered that I saw no need to pay attention to power, but even as I said this I could hear the hollowness of my words.

Zoughbi's challenge stayed with me because I was beginning to have doubts about whether our dialogue processes could deliver the results we were promising. I was seeing many examples of seemingly successful processes producing unsuccessful results. A team of leaders from across a given system would come together to change that system, and they would connect deeply with one another, with their context, and with what was needed of them; but once the dust settled, the system would remain unchanged. Something was missing from our theory and practice. Through a series of experiences over the years that followed, I gradually came to understand what this was.

In 2006, I went to the Philippines to facilitate a workshop of national leaders from the government of President Gloria Macapagal-Arroyo, from the opposition, and from business, media, and nongovernmental organizations. The opposition had accused Arroyo of electoral fraud and considered her government to be illegitimate. Amidst this institutional instability, the country was reeling from social decay and from violent insurrection and counterinsurrection. The workshop was convened by leaders of the Catholic Church who sensed an opening to unblock the country's tense standoff.

The workshop went well. It was organized elegantly; all the invitees came and stayed; and the conversation was frank and touched on many key issues. On a series of flip-chart pages, the participants assembled an insightful synthesis of the core dynamics in the current Filipino reality. When they looked at what they had written, they were taken aback by the reality that none of them wanted but that all of them had contributed to creating. Out of this realization, they agreed to undertake six joint initiatives, including a delicate process to review the legitimacy of the president.

The day after the workshop ended, I left Manila feeling proud of what we had accomplished. So I was stunned to learn, by the time my plane landed back in Boston, that the participants had already been denounced and denounced one another in the newspapers, and the whole exercise had collapsed. One week later, the church abandoned the effort as too controversial to be productive.

The tentative, hasty unity of the separated that we accomplished within the workshop fell apart outside the workshop. During the dialogue, we focused most of our attention on unity, not on the different and conflicting positions and interests of the participating groups. This left the participants vulnerable to attack by their own colleagues for selling out to the other groups, leaving the workshop agreements vulnerable to the collapse that immediately occurred.

The acrimonious collapse of the workshop agreements produced not merely a failure, but a regression. The goodwill we constructed, the resources we expended, and the hopes we raised were all lost. Filipino intellectual and activist Nicanor Perlas, who had observed this effort from outside with growing concern, said to me later that as a result of several such failures Filipinos had become more cynical and polarized, and the situation in the country had worsened.

The hint that Zoughbi had given me—not to ignore power—had been apt. I was starting to see the significance of King's warning that "love without power is sentimental and anemic." It turned out that King's formulation understated the danger.

In 2007, I visited Colombia, where ten years before I had worked on a scenario project called Destino Colombia. This exercise, aimed at looking for a way out of the country's long-running conflict, had brought together leaders of most of the armed actors (the military, paramilitary, and guerrillas) plus a diverse team of politicians, businesspeople, and representatives of civil society.[14] Our workshops in 1997 had been the first (and to date the only) time such a mixed group had come together in an extended dialogue, and these encounters had been intense, friendly, and creative. The team had ended up agreeing on four scenarios as to how the country's future might unfold, and they had communicated these stories widely, at large public meetings, on all the television channels, in all the newspapers—but with little apparent impact. One of the project organizers, Manuel José Carvajal, told me that he thought their mistake might have been to exclude from the team any members of the government of President Ernesto Samper, on the grounds that Samper was suspected of having received money from drug traffickers and was therefore a polarizing figure. Carvajal characterized the considered stance of the organizers as "aseptic." My interpretation of this story was that, if we are afraid of being contaminated by the dirty realities of power, we will fail to effect social change.

I was surprised, then, on my return to Colombia, to hear Bogotá politician and intellectual Antanas Mockus's alternative perspective on the impact that Destino Colombia had had on the country. His view gave me further insight into the risks of love without power.

During the 1997 project, the team had articulated four scenarios. The first, "When the Sun Rises We'll See," was a prophetic warning of the chaos that would result if Colombians failed to address their tough challenges. The second, "A Bird in the Hand Is Worth Two in the Bush," was a story of a negotiated compromise with the guerrillas; Samper's successor, President Andrés

Pastrana, tried and failed to achieve such a settlement. The third scenario, "Forward March!," was a story of how the government, supported by a population frustrated with the continuing violence and operating from the principle that "a hard problem requires a hard solution," implements a policy of crushing the guerrillas militarily, thus enforcing peace on the country. Pastrana's successor, President Álvaro Uribe, was elected in 2002 on just such a wave of popular frustration. The fourth scenario, "In Unity Lies Strength," was a story of a bottom-up transformation of the country's mentality towards greater mutual respect and cooperation.

Antanas Mockus's hypothesis was that some businesspeople and landowners, having concluded that Forward March! was the best option for themselves and for the country, had suggested it as a blueprint to the Uribe government. This government had in fact (and to widespread acclaim) implemented just such an aggressive crackdown. Mockus's inference was, "We must not fix our attention only on the conviviality of such dialogue processes. We must not forget the harsher external world where scenarios can be chosen to guide action."[15]

Thus love without attention to or transformation of power can be, not merely sentimental and anemic, but reinforcing of the capacity of the already powerful to act recklessly and abusively. Brazilian educator Paolo Freire warns that "'Washing one's hands' of the conflict between the powerful and the powerless means to side with the powerful, not to be neutral."[16] Ignoring power is evidence either of naïveté or cunning.

A year after Colombia, in 2008, I was invited by Elena Díez to return to Guatemala for the tenth anniversary of Visión Guatemala. I was excited to see my friends again, but also concerned by what I was hearing about current events: a deepening economic crisis; increasingly serious security threats from organized

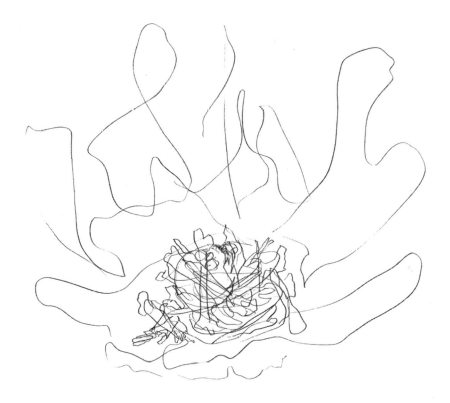

when my feelings extend only to me

crime and elements of the military; and disappointment in the new government, led by our Visión Guatemala teammate, now president, Álvaro Colom. And I was keenly interested in how the work that we had all done together—which I had written about so enthusiastically in *Solving Tough Problems*—was now being seen.

In the decade since we had launched the project, a lot had happened. Guatemala was not in a stable, steady state: the country was being swept by in-and-out international flows of money, migrants, businesspeople, drugs, and criminals. Everyone I spoke to agreed that Visión Guatemala and the many other dialogues it had inspired had strengthened the capacity of Guatemalans to address these severe social challenges—to resolve their conflicts—openly and democratically. In particular, these efforts had helped them move beyond their previous national default mode for dealing with such challenges: authoritarian power-over.

The shortcoming of these dialogues, however, was that the results they produced were in general not institutionalized and therefore (as in my Filipino experience) did not last. One important exception was the successful implementation of those parts of the Peace Accords that had been acted upon and monitored by national government and United Nations structures. Many of the dialogues produced new spaces and relationships across ideological, class, and ethnic lines; new connections and renewed unity; and, from these, new insights and intentions. But these alone were insufficient to create new realities.

Eduardo Gonzalez, a member of Visión Guatemala and a banker, told me that the elite of neighboring El Salvador had moved further than their Guatemalan counterparts in responding to the challenges posed by left-wing guerrillas and the social forces they were manifesting because their interdependence was more obvious. "In Guatemala," he said, "the war was fought mostly in the countryside. But in El Salvador, the war came into the capital city, where it could not be ignored." People will change their behavior only when they believe that what they are doing can't work anymore. Often, in order for this to happen, "the war has to come into the city": the problem has to be felt strongly and closely enough so that it cannot be ignored.

The truth that was inconvenient for the elite in Guatemala (as elsewhere), who exercised both power-to and power-over, was that to acknowledge fully the unity that the dialogues uncovered would imply taking action to empower others and thereby diminish their own privilege. Most of the time, the elite in Guatemala did not volunteer to take this action, and so the intentions conceived in the voluntary dialogues were stillborn.

Clara Arenas, another member of Visión Guatemala, is the director of an influential left-wing research and advocacy organization. Her long history in social change work has left her skeptical about the prospect of elites spontaneously ceding their power-over. She once wrote to me:

> I see a certain naïveté in your vision of a balance between power and love, in which things can be improved leaving everyone satisfied. How can that be? In a context of great imbalance or inequity, as in Guatemala, how can poverty be uprooted without some sectors of society (of power, of course) being very dissatisfied? It is their economic interests which will be affected. I think that balance and satisfaction for all are possible in the realm of discourse, but not when you go down to "real" politics in a context of enormous inequality.
>
> This imbalance between discourse and "real" politics reminds me of what American anthropologist Charles Hale has said about racism in Guatemala. According to Hale, the discourse of the *ladinos*, people of mixed ancestry, from the town of Chimaltenango is all for equality, universal rights, anti-racism, etc., but at the same time their practice does not concede an inch of

their privileges, which stem from their position in the racial hierarchy. He calls this "racial ambivalence." In the end, ambivalence works in favor of the status quo.

Your analysis also reminds me of a phrase of Franz Hinkelammert (a German theologian living in Costa Rica) that "assassination is suicide," meaning that those who hold power and exert repression should know that, in the end, that road leads to their own killing. This would mean that, for their own good, the powerful and wealthy should learn love.[17]

When I saw Arenas during our anniversary meetings, she told me that she and her colleagues had become so frustrated with the nondelivery of the many Guatemalan dialogues that they had taken out a newspaper advertisement saying they would no longer participate in these processes. They did this because the government expected that the organizations participating in dialogues would meanwhile desist from organizing strikes and marches and other forms of popular resistance. Love without power—unity without space for self-realization—is not merely sentimental and anemic but is deceitfully reinforcing of the status quo.

Love creates opening, potential, and opportunity, but power is required for these to be tested and realized. Dialogue that does not acknowledge and work with power therefore cannot create new social realities. On the contrary, it can only re-create and reinforce current realities. Paul Tillich recognizes this need of love for power, but argues for differentiating between power-to that destroys oppressive institutions and power-over that destroys people: "Love, through compulsory power, must destroy what is against love. But love cannot destroy him who acts against love. Even when destroying his work it does not destroy him. The compulsory element of power is the tragic aspect of love. It represents a price that must be paid for the reunion of the separated."[18] Creating new social realities requires both a loving drive to unite and a powerful drive to realize this unity. Exercising power with love requires effecting systemic change without destroying what we are trying to nurture.

I wasn't expecting or looking out for this degenerative side of love, or for the dependence of generative love on power. So it wasn't until I had seen and thought about this phenomenon many times in different forms—both personal and professional   that I understood its significance.

Love without power is unity that constrains or undermines self-realization. For most of the time I had been in London, I had lived alone, had only a few friends, and focused mostly on my work. In moving to Cape Town, I entered a big bustling family and a close-knit community, which I found wonderful—and also constraining, of me and of others. This contrast between my old and new lives allowed me to see the often subtle and unconscious ways that connectedness and mutual responsibility ("if you loved us, you would . . .") can not only nurture but also impede self-development.

In working on social change, love without power manifests in a feel-good connection that is impotent: it does not and cannot produce real change. Otto Scharmer points out that the practice of what he calls "downloading," of reenacting the status quo by saying what we always say and doing what we always do, produces a polite, conflict-avoiding, counterfeit wholeness.[19] We may believe that we have transcended our self when we are united with others or with our higher self, but often we are experiencing only a counterfeit projection of our smaller self or ego. Hidden beneath the surface of counterfeit love without power is a self-deceiving and self-serving power without love.

Love without power is dangerous because power is never absent—only sometimes concealed. My wife Dorothy once surprised me by saying that many South African blacks distrust liberal English-speaking whites, whom they suspect of being closet racists, more than they distrust overtly racist Afrikaans-speaking ones. "Wouldn't you prefer," I asked, "that no matter what someone thinks about you, they at least be polite?" "No," she replied, "racism is easier to fight when it is out in the open." Concealed power is harder to deal with than overt power.

This problem of love that conceals power often shows up in the helping professions, where power is always present but frequently undiscussable. Psychologist James Hillman writes about this in a way that accords with my own different experiences of power in different sectors:

> Why are the conflicts about power so ruthless—less so in business and politics, where they are an everyday matter, than in the idealistic professions of clergy, medicine, the arts, teaching and nursing? In business and politics, it seems, there is less idealism and more sense of shadow. Power is not repressed but lived with as a daily companion; moreover, it is not declared to be the enemy of love. So long as the notion of power is itself corrupted by a romantic opposition with love, power will indeed corrupt. The corruption begins not in power, but in the ignorance about it.[20]

A management consultant once told me that of all the organizational change projects she had worked on, the hardest had been in the health sector because the frequent injunction "Let's not forget the patients" serves in practice not to inspire change, but to divert attention from real conflicts of interest and power. An Anglican priest who had worked on the problem of sexual abuse by clergy once suggested to me that the root of this problem was clergy who were uncomfortable with their own power and so used it unwisely. And as a facilitator, I have noticed that people are most aggrieved when they feel manipulated by me: when they think that their voice and power are being ignored or twisted in the supposed service of a larger or higher unity. The most degenerative, perverted form of love is that which denies or represses or covers up self-realizing power.

I experienced the pain of this power-denying love myself in an early meeting of our Global Leadership Initiative team. Ten of us spent a week at a retreat center on a wild mountain property in Colorado. A particular tension ran through this meeting. Most of the team thought it was essential that we articulate and take a stand for the underlying connectedness of all being, for retreating into wilderness as the way to access that connectedness, and for the centrality of this access to addressing the world's toughest social challenges. I was in the minority in doubting these premises: I was not confident that a deep felt sense of connectedness was sufficient to achieve the results we wanted, and my own retreat experiences had neither revealed to me this deep connectedness nor much shifted my actions.

My doubts were magnified one morning when a teacher from the retreat center took us all on a walk around the property to show us some rock formations that he said had powerful energetic properties. At one formation after another, my colleagues sat or held their hands as the teacher demonstrated, and marveled at the sensations of connectedness they experienced. But when I approached the rocks, I didn't notice any sensations. I was torn between my need to belong and to unite with these, my closest colleagues and friends, and my need to be true to my own different experience. I felt subjugated.

Solomon Asch, a social psychologist who studied agreement-forming processes in the 1950s, says, "Consensus is valid only to the extent to which each individual asserts his own relation to the facts and retains his individuality. There can be no genuine agreement unless each adheres to the testimony of his experience and steadfastly maintains his hold on reality."[21] A hegemonic doctrine of boundary-less unity that denies each person his or

her own boundaries is a form of love without power that prevents valid consensus and therefore cannot be sustained.

POWER IS WHAT MAKES LOVE GENERATIVE

Based on these experiences, then, here is how I understand the
nature of love and its relationship to power. Love has two sides,
one generative and the other degenerative. Our love is generative when it empowers us and others: when it helps us, individually and collectively, to complete ourselves and grow. Our love is
degenerative—sentimental and anemic, or worse—when it over-
looks or denies or suffocates power.

the whole cosmos works into birth

3
The Dilemma of Power and Love

*P*OWER WITHOUT LOVE is reckless and abusive, or worse, and love without power is sentimental and anemic, or worse. We can see both of these degenerative forms in our world, in our work, and in our selves. Choosing either power or love is always a mistake. How then can we exercise power and love together?

In answering this question, I was inspired by Cambridge University management researcher Charles Hampden-Turner's study of dilemmas. I met Hampden-Turner when we were both working in Shell's global planning department. Under Arie de Geus's leadership, the department was a model of open, collegial inquiry, with outsiders such as Hampden-Turner, Joseph Jaworski, and me hired to inject fresh perspectives into the company's thinking. So I was intrigued to learn that, of the twenty or so internal papers on planning methodology that the department had published, one of them was considered so provocative that it was left off the list of papers and circulated only in underground, *samizdat* copies. This was Hampden-Turner's paper on dilemmas that he had observed in Shell's culture.

In Hampden-Turner's work on dilemmas at Shell and elsewhere, he unveils the enduring, red-hot tensions at the heart of a social system. His names for several frequently occurring dilemmas seem innocuous: pluralism versus centralism, technical excellence versus customer focus, competition versus cooperation.[1] But to be caught on the horns of such a dilemma is to risk being torn apart.

In this particular sense, *dilemma* refers to a challenge that consists of two propositions, each of which, if pursued too aggressively, will disturb the health of the whole and therefore needs to be balanced by the other. In Greek mythology, sailors in the Strait of Messina had to navigate between the twin perils of rocks on one side and a whirlpool on the other. I see power and love as just such a dilemma: to choose one and deny the other is to place ourselves in peril. But, as Hampden-Turner writes, "it is all very fine to say that you will 'steer between' values that are in tension, or will 'combine' them. In practice this is quite difficult and needs particular ways of thinking and acting which are not the usual ways."[2]

Hampden-Turner offers a clue as to how to reconcile power and love in practice: "What makes contrasting values *seem* so oppositional is that both are presented to us at one moment in time. In reality, time is used to mediate these contrasts."[3] I see learning to employ both power and love to be like learning to walk on two legs. We can't walk on only one leg, just as we can't address our toughest social challenges only with power or only with love. But walking on two legs does not mean either moving them both at the same time or always being stably balanced. On the contrary, it means moving first one leg and then the other and always being *out* of balance—or more precisely, always being in dynamic balance.

The key to walking on two legs is that even when we are focusing on one, we must not forget the other. This is like the circular symbol for yin and yang, in which the black yin part contains a small white yang dot and vice versa. Paul Tillich puts it this way: "Constructive social ethics presuppose that one is aware of the element of love in structures of power and the element of power without which love becomes chaotic surrender."[4]

There is a scene in the movie *The Wizard of Oz* that presents a memorable image of learning to walk. The Scarecrow gets down

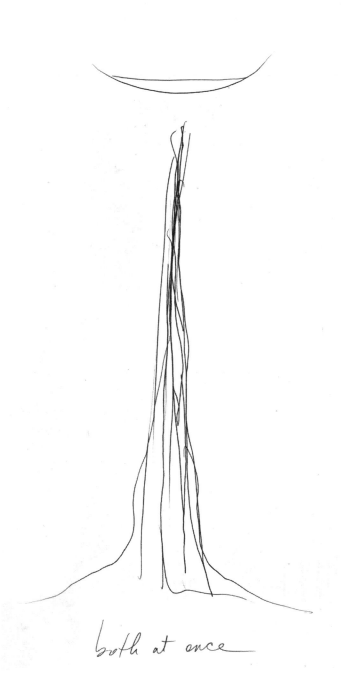

both at once

from the pole on which he has been stuck and tries to stand up on his floppy legs and move forward. First he falls down, then he stumbles dangerously, and finally he walks, even skips, fluidly and happily.

We can see these same three states when we employ our power and love to try to shift a stuck social situation. When our power and love are disconnected, we fall down; when our power is stronger than our love, or vice versa, we stumble dangerously; and when we are able to balance and shift between power and love, so that the two phenomena become one, we walk fluidly.

I have observed, in others and in myself, all three of the states. They form a progression: when we are falling, we are unable to co-create new social realities; when we are stumbling, we are unstably able; and when we are walking, we are confidently able. This does not mean that we can always progress linearly from one state to the next; often, lacking awareness or capacity, we regress. Certainly I have sometimes progressed and sometimes regressed, which is why I have related the stories in this book in a non-chronological order.

In the following three chapters, I describe falling, stumbling, and walking. I have chosen stories from my own project experiences to illustrate the external and internal dynamics of these states: from India in "Falling," from Israel and South Africa in "Stumbling," and from Europe and the Americas in "Walking." I am not saying that these projects were generally or always characterized by these states; often painful falling leads to profound learning and to vigorous walking, and often overconfident walking leads to arrogant inattention and to catastrophic falling. Nor am I saying that these countries are generally or always characterized by these states; we can be in any state in any context. I am saying that in trying to effect social change, our capacity to take a next step that will move us forward depends on our capacity to recognize the state of our power and love. This simple three-part framework and these illustrative stories can help us recognize where we are and what we can do next.

4
Falling

$\mathcal{W}$E FALL DOWN PAINFULLY when, like a scarecrow or a marionette, our two legs become disconnected from each other. We fall down when our power and our love become polarized: when our power is without love and our love is without power. We fall down when, intentionally or unintentionally, we make the elementary and common error of treating the relationship between power and love, which is a dilemma, as if it was a choice.

IMPROVING CHILD NUTRITION IN INDIA

By 2003, Generon was working confidently on implementing its Global Leadership Initiative. We wanted to address some of the world's toughest challenges and to develop and demonstrate our change lab approach. That summer we got a great opportunity: a European food company executive asked us to help him organize a project to find and implement initiatives to reduce child malnutrition in India.

As we started to develop this project, we discovered that in the field of international public health, India stands out as a glaring and distressing anomaly. Fifty-five million, or 43 percent, of Indian children under five years old are underweight (this is one of the highest rates in the world), and 35 percent of all the underweight children in the world are in India.[1] Furthermore, in

57

spite of having one of the world's largest government programs aimed at solving this problem (wiith a budget of over $1 billion per year), the Indian rate of child malnutrition has come down only slowly.

There is a provocative tautology in systems thinking: "The system is perfectly designed to produce the results it is now producing."[2] So the Indian "social-cultural-political-economic-nutritional system" was perfectly designed to produce—that is, was functioning in a way that reliably resulted in—43 percent child malnutrition. Peace researcher Johan Galtung refers to such systems as characterized by "structural violence": violence produced indirectly and unintentionally that is, from the perspective of its victims, just as real as if it had been produced directly and intentionally.[3] The objective of our project was to find a nonviolent way to change this system, so that it produced better nutritional results.

In the first months of 2004, we spent weeks in India talking with people working in hospitals, government departments, research institutions, companies, and nongovernmental organizations (NGOs). The child malnutrition situation was dynamically, socially, and generatively complex, and the people we met had many different understandings of what the essence of the problem was and therefore of where the solution could be found. Their various understandings included poverty and underemployment; artificially high food prices; poor diets, health care, or education; poorly functioning and corrupt government programs; missing or misplaced private sector involvement; disempowerment of women and girl children; and caste and religious divisions.

What struck me in meeting these people was how knowledgeable and committed and full of power-to they were individually, and yet how disconnected, even alienated, they were from one another. This seemed to be a more promising situation than the opposite, which I had seen elsewhere: a group of poorly informed and uncommitted people who were already working closely with one another. I was hopeful that we could achieve real breakthroughs, if only these outstanding, separated individuals could be united.

Almost everyone we met said that child malnutrition was a real problem that should and could be addressed. (Prime Minister Manmohan Singh was later quoted in the newspaper as calling it "a national shame.") Nobody said that the situation would fix itself and that we should just let it be. The Indian economy was booming, Indian companies were becoming more important internationally, and Indians seemed confident that this was a problem that together they could solve.

I asked businessman Arun Maira, who has pioneered multistakeholder dialogue processes in India, what he saw as the essence of the innovation that this project was attempting to create.[4] "You have to remember," he replied, "that most of the time, when a group of stakeholder leaders enter a dialogue, every one of them believes that if only the other ones would change what they are thinking and doing, then the problem would be solved. But it is not possible that it is all the fault of others! The real innovation here is that we are inviting stakeholder leaders to reflect on how they might need to change what they themselves are thinking and doing."

The project was frustratingly difficult and slow to organize. We suffered months of misunderstandings and mismatches among the growing cast of participating business, government, and civil society organizations. Eventually, after more than two years, we were ready to go. We named our initiative the Bhavishya Alliance: *bhavishya* is the Sanskrit word for "future." We set ourselves an ambitious objective: to contribute to India's meeting its Millennium Development Goal of reducing the rate of child malnutrition by 50 percent by 2015. We would begin our work in the western state of Maharashtra (population 100 million) and its capital city Mumbai.

Over the long back-and-forth among the partner organizations, we settled on a tightly orchestrated project design. Each partner would appoint one or several staff members to join the

Bhavishya Lab Team. In order to move quickly and stay focused, this team would work together full time for eight weeks over three months. During this time, they would go through the three movements of the change lab: co-sensing by immersing in the system that was producing malnutrition; co-presencing by retreating together in nature; and then co-realizing by rapidly prototyping, with potential partners, models of possible initiatives to reduce malnutrition. The lab would be facilitated by three of us from Generon with five Indian colleagues. A group of Champions—top executives from each of the partner organizations, the bosses of the team members—would provide ongoing feedback and, in the eighth week, judge the lab team's proposed initiatives. Three executives from partner organizations would be seconded to co-manage the alliance, and one company would contribute a large open-plan working space, plus support staff, in a suburb of Mumbai. All in all, we had a lot of resources— a diverse team of fifty-two people and the focused attention of their twenty-six organizations, plus a staff of sixteen—to put behind this effort. We were confident that we had a good plan.

The Bhavishya Alliance was full of love and full of power. The essential logic of the project was a courageous and heart-felt drive to unite the separated: privileged with underprivileged people; international with Indian institutions; and Indian government with corporate with civil society actors. Many individuals involved had devoted their lives to helping poor women and children. Generon's Global Leadership Initiative and change lab approach had at their methodological core a focus on uniting diverse stakeholder leaders with one another, with their context, and with their own highest potentials.

At the same time, the alliance was full of forceful individual and organizational drives to self-realization. It brought together a large and diverse group of action-oriented and ambitious players. The power differences and dynamics were complex: between enormous government bureaucracies and small NGOs, between experts and novices, between funders and recipients, between bosses and staff, between men and women, between foreign consultants and Indians, and between all of us in Bhavishya and the malnourished children and families and communities we were intending to help.

In April 2006, we launched the lab. The stakes and expectations of all the participants were high, and everybody was impatient to get going and see results. The compressed timetable for the lab meant many long days and long weeks. When we were in Mumbai, we all met together in our open-plan office; the out-of-town lab team members lived in a nearby hotel, and the staff stayed in four apartments in a single building. In subteams we traveled around the city and across the state. "The design of the Lab," wrote Gomathy Balasubramanian, Mia Eisenstadt, and Zaid Hassan in a reflection on the project, "in sheer size and scale, resembled a high-speed, high-risk moon shot. The need for speed overrode most other considerations."[5] The lab team spent one spacious and fruitful week on a retreat together in a beautiful forest in the Himalayas, northeast of Maharashtra. This exception proved the rule: the change lab was a pressure cooker.

When I look back at my experience of Bhavishya, I can make out (among other patterns) two underlying dynamics. On the one hand, I experienced that we often exercised love without paying attention to power. For example, in our design and facilitation, we emphasized the horizontal sharing and unifying of perspectives and neglected the expertise and authority of the more senior members of the lab team. "Treating participants as equals," the project reflection says, "resulted in many interactions between participants being status transactions, with uncertainties in power being constantly (re)negotiated."[6] What the team most wanted to do during the first week of the lab was for the experts among them to make didactic presentations to the whole group, but the facilitators decided that this wouldn't fit with our dialogic methodology. This decision left the team feeling disrespected and disempowered.

There were many areas of disagreement and conflict within the team. Most of these arose from the fundamentally different mental models, among the government officials, corporate managers, NGO activists, and facilitators, about what constituted viable and legitimate practices for effecting social change. These disagreements were sometimes aired, but they were never resolved, and gradually they became undiscussable. In the fourth week, the most junior, female member of the staff team said in a plenary session that she was aware of a conflict occurring in the group. The person chairing the session, the most senior, male government official on the lab team, declared, "There is no conflict here!" The staff member was silenced, and over the remaining four weeks, she never, ever spoke in plenary again. In the interest of preserving unity, we prevented self-realization—and so obstructed creativity and change.

The work of the team also suffered because the self-realizing drive of some members had been overridden. Rather than volunteering, they had been instructed by their organizations to participate in the lab. The project reflection says, "One explanation for the number of conflicts that arose over the course of the Lab was the presence of participants who had not decided to undertake the process of their own free will. Because there was no legitimate route to 'exit' the project, these participants had very little to lose in objecting to the process. This policy of 'inclusion at all costs' is incongruent with the conditions for the emergence of collective intelligence."[7]

The focus of the international organizers of the Bhavishya Alliance on the project's loving ambition obscured the fundamental power dynamics we were enacting. The project was initiated, funded, and managed mostly by foreigners, and it was not until one year after the end of the change lab that the governance and leadership of the alliance was taken over by Indians. So

during the change lab itself, in the absence of an explicit agreement as to how power would be wielded and decisions would be made, the de facto pattern was that decisions were made by the most closely involved senior foreigners. In frequently exhorting one another to rise above our own interests and to "remember the children," we denied the reality of our power in the system.

Our accelerated change lab process emphasized the generation of breakthrough initiatives through collaboration within the trisector lab team and deferred until the post-lab piloting phase the practical questions of how these initiatives would be funded, staffed, and implemented. We were betting that the insight and commitment built up within the lab team would be sufficient to bring along the Champions and their institutions and resources. At the conclusion of the retreat in the fourth week, one of the NGO members of the lab team expressed his concern about this approach: "Today is the twenty-fifth day, so that's good. But on the fiftieth day I won't be happy to say the same thing again, about what I learned about myself. So let's do something very fruitful now!"[8]

The authors of the project reflection also commented on our inattention to power:

> The sociologist Ulrich Beck makes the case that "one could almost say, whenever nobody is talking about power, that is where it unquestionably exists, at once secure and great in its unquestionability. Wherever power is the subject of discussion, that is the start of its decline." The point, of course, is not a decline of power for its own sake. Rather, it is important that participants do not feel that they are merely cogs in a process that is beyond their control, subject to hidden power dynamics. Instead, organizers need to ensure that the group has real agency in the design and structure of the change lab process. When power dynamics are explicitly discussed, the group can come to terms with its

own collective identity and relational agency. When power differentials and dynamics are masked, there is a risk that both individuals and the collective will become politically disenfranchised and essentially ineffective. The change lab as a vehicle for systemic change will only succeed when the power dynamics present within the larger system are consciously addressed.[9]

The second, polar opposite dynamic I experienced in Bhavishya was that we often exercised power without paying attention to love. For example, the NGO activists on the lab team were worried about the involvement of corporations in child nutrition. The provision of enriched prepared foods that are nutritious but that undermine the self-sufficiency and hence the capacity for self-realization of recipients was of particular concern. The activists also had another, related concern: the large-scale approach that national, state, and local governments and aid agencies typically take to addressing child malnutrition entails power over communities and families. We once had a heated debate about whether it is right for government health workers to vaccinate children by force over the objections of their parents. One of the most heartfelt moments of self-reflection came when, during a meeting of the whole lab team, a woman from UNICEF burst out, "Do we really make a difference in the community? Because I am also a person with a development background, and I've seen that we have done harm. Let me tell you it's all driven! It's NGO-driven, it's government-driven, it's World Bank-driven, it's UNICEF-driven!"[10]

Generon's Global Leadership Initiative had slipped into a similar pattern of driving our own projects, of realizing our agenda, in a way that often was not requested by or responsive to—that was largely disconnected from—the people we said we were trying to serve. Our vision of initiating projects that would contribute to solving ten of the world's toughest problems verged on grandiose, missionary power-over.

A structural feature of the change lab design in Bhavishya was the two tiers of participation: the full-time members of the lab team and the Champions who visited the lab four times over the eight weeks. The Champions had the most power to make decisions about the implementation of the initiatives, but they also had the most attenuated connection and commitment to one another and to the content and spirit of the alliance's work. One member of the alliance staff said to me two years later, "The Champions said that they wanted us to achieve breakthrough innovations, but time and again they prevented us from deviating from the usual way of doing things. They were like owners of an ocean-going boat who are not willing to let it get out of sight of the shore."

Several members of the staff team, of which I was a leader, said that their experience in Bhavishya left them feeling disempowered. Family systems therapist Edwin Friedman suggests that this is a typical symptom of leadership characterized by love without power:

> In any type of institution whatsoever, when a self-directed, imaginative, energetic, or creative member is being consistently frustrated and sabotaged rather than encouraged and supported, what will turn out to be true one hundred percent of the time, regardless of whether the disrupters are supervisors, subordinates, or peers, is that the person at the very top of that institution is a *peace-monger.* By that I mean a highly anxious risk-avoider, someone who is more concerned with good feelings than with progress, someone whose life revolves around the axis of consensus.[11]

As the eighth-week deadline to deliver the initiatives approached and the fear and pressure increased, my own way of leading narrowed, hardened, and became characterized by power without love. I became more distant and isolated from both the lab and staff teams. My understanding of what was going on and my capacity to deal with it intelligently diminished. I thought that if I held on more tightly and pushed harder, I could get the lab over the goal line. Halfway through the lab, when it was already becoming apparent that the work was not unfolding according to our plan and schedule, some of the staff suggested that we go back to the sponsors and negotiate a delay of a few months in our delivery deadline. But I, afraid that we and I would be seen to have failed, vetoed the suggestion.

These two poles of love without power and power without love, in the project and in me, clashed cataclysmically on the final day of the lab. The lab team proposed to the Champions four innovative initiatives that they believed could, if piloted and developed and scaled up successfully, contribute to meeting the alliance's ambitious objectives for reducing child malnutrition. These initiatives had been generated through the team's intense interaction with each other and with the stakeholders we had worked with over the course of the lab. They also involved effecting radical changes to the "malnutrition system," in particular a shift in control away from the state government and towards local communities.

The members of the lab team had pushed themselves hard, had survived many arguments, and were exhausted but satisfied with where they had arrived. Most of them were committed, notwithstanding the risks to their own careers, to staying involved in Bhavishya and working on the implementation of the initiatives.

But the Champions saw things differently. Many of them were critical of our proposals and doubted whether they were sound or viable. One of them thought that our work was poorly thought through and stepped in to call for an immediate meeting of the

Champions without the lab team. By the end of the day, almost none of the lab team's work had been approved. The lab team felt bewildered and distressed. I felt devastated.

Later I told this story to businessman and Buddhist teacher Michael Chender. He commented, "When you get very close to the heart of the system, that is when the devils will appear. By devils I mean the system's strongest and trickiest defenders: its auto-immune system. If you aren't prepared for this, then you will be overwhelmed, and your efforts to change the system will fail."

In the weeks that followed this Champions' meeting, the lab disintegrated. Team members went back to their previous jobs, with only a few remaining engaged with the alliance. The staff team, hurt, spent days trying to understand what had happened and why. Then we also went our separate ways; the Generon team left India and returned home.

Under Bhavishya's rigid constraints and high pressure, then, the lab had come apart. Every one of us was doing the best he or she could, but nonetheless our work did not unfold as we had planned. One reason was that many of us—certainly I—had become afraid, and as we became afraid we each reverted to our own simpler and more familiar ways of operating. Some of us had focused on love and some on power; a few of us (too few) had focused on both. Our love and our power had become separated and polarized, and we fell down.

During one of the earlier breaks in the change lab, the staff had held a three-day meeting, facilitated by South African psychologist Myrna Lewis, to reflect on what was happening in the project and within our team. Lewis looks at members of a group as part of a field that extends between and within and beyond them. Rather than ignoring differences and conflicts, she amplifies and polarizes them, so that the group can see the multiple perspectives, or "roles," in the field, including within each of us.[12]

This approach to conflict startled me. For years I had been working with the approach advocated by facilitator Marvin Weisbord: "We neither avoid nor confront the extremes that are in conflict. Rather, we put our energy into staking out the widest common ground all can stand upon without forcing or compromising."[13] I had been focusing on discovering and articulating the common or larger interest of all parties. I had been assuming that what was common was more important than what was different.

Myrna Lewis thinks that working with difference and conflict can be a doorway into a broader and deeper understanding of the system as a whole and of ourselves—and is therefore a capacity that needs to be cultivated. She seeks to prevent the formation of a false consensus that will inevitably be undermined and is therefore unsustainable. She believes in dealing with conflict early, before it degenerates and becomes violent.

When during this staff meeting Lewis heard about the tensions and conflicts within Bhavishya, she made an incisive diagnosis:

> It is inevitable that this group would have to deal with the challenges raised by differences in power. You have placed yourselves right in the middle of the field of one of the biggest power differences in the world: that between well-off, healthy professionals on the one hand, and weak, malnourished children on the other. So of course all of the difficult dynamics between helper and helpee, up and down, powerful and powerless, oppressor and oppressed, are showing up within your project as well. At the same time, the fact that your intended beneficiaries are not directly involved in the Lab means that you are not working with this polarity directly, and so the potential for you to achieve a creative breakthrough through working with this conflict is limited.

Lewis's work with our staff team was illuminating. But as the pressure ratcheted up, we did not have the presence of mind to work with these conflictual dynamics. Instead these dynamics created increasing dysfunction.

The day after the staff meeting with Lewis, I had a private counseling session with her. I was shocked to see that the same perverse powerful/powerless field dynamics at play in and around Bhavishya were also playing out within me. There was a powerful, strong, and grown-up part of me, confident, arrogant, focused on getting the job done. In the pressure cooker of Bhavishya, this part of me, increasingly desperate to keep the lab on track and fearful of losing control and being humiliated, became increasingly reckless and abusive. And there was also a powerless, malnourished, and childlike part of me, fearful of being hurt, needy, and desperate for support and connection. In the lab, terrified of being abandoned, unloved, this part of me became increasingly sentimental and anemic. The polarization and conflict between power and love was alive within me.

<hr />

After the Bhavishya Lab had fallen down and the dust had settled, the staff who remained picked themselves up, reflected on what happened, got back to work, and reconceived and rebuilt the alliance. Over the years that followed, they strengthened the Bhavishya platform for collaboration among government departments, businesses, and NGOs. From this platform they developed and implemented a new series of innovative trisector initiatives aimed at reducing child malnutrition in India.[14]

In the meantime, Generon fell down and so did I. We had invested years of effort and a lot of our reputation in the Global Leadership Initiative in general and Bhavishya in particular. The unraveling of Bhavishya was painful and embarrassing for everyone, but especially for those of us who had been in India and for me as our project leader.

This unraveling also widened the split in our Generon team that had first appeared at our Colorado meeting five years earlier, hardening a polarization that mirrored the one in Bhavishya. We emphasized, externally and internally, the primary importance of the drive to unity, denying and papering over our differences. At the same time, the divergent trajectories of the partners weakened the connections among us. Every one of us was doing the best he or she could, but nonetheless our work did not unfold as we had planned. By the end of 2006, Generon had split into two successor firms.

This whole experience distressed and sobered me. I had seen in my own behavior both of these degenerative forms: a conflict-averse love that disempowered others and denied my own power, and a power-over that denied and broke my connection to others. An Indian colleague once said to me, "Pain is our guru— our teacher." The pain of this fall pushed me to look deeper into myself and into what it takes to effect social change.

How to fall

For political or philosophical or psychological reasons, we often mistakenly choose to pay attention either only to power or only to love. Most of us prefer one of these drives over the other, or deny one in favor of the other. Even if we understand the need to employ both drives, when under pressure and frightened and constrained, we often revert to our habitual choice of either power or love.

When in these ways our power and our love become polarized, both manifest their degenerative, fallen forms. Our power becomes reckless and abusive, and our love becomes sentimental and anemic.

What must we do when we find ourselves falling down? Above all we must refuse to choose between power and love. We must keep both drives in view and in hand. In this way they will remain connected, and each will make the other more generative.

rising

One way to make both power and love visible is to inquire explicitly after them—to ensure that both are acknowledged and discussable rather than denied and undiscussable. We must, with others, ask about our situation: Where is the power here? What is each of the actors (including ourselves) trying to achieve and realize? What are their positions, needs, and interests? Who is employing what kind of power-to and power-over? Whose voices are being heard and whose are not? And where is the love here? How are the actors separated, and how are they unified? What is it that is driven to being reunited? What is being kept united that is not driven to be?

Consultant Louis van der Merwe taught me that in starting any social change initiative, we need to keep in mind that "the pattern is set at the beginning." In particular, we need to ask, Which systemic patterns of power and love—of realization and nonrealization, of connection and nonconnection—are we interrupting or reinforcing? If the patterns we set intentionally or unintentionally increase or sustain the polarization of power and love, we will fall down.

We all fall down, sometimes when we are inattentive and sometimes when the terrain we are traversing is treacherous. Falling down hurts, but we can learn from it. Falling down signals to us that we need to reflect on what we have been doing and why and with what effect. Then we must pick ourselves up and, with greater attentiveness, try to move forward again.

5
Stumbling

*W*E STUMBLE WHEN one of our legs is stronger than the other. We stumble when our power dominates our love, or our love dominates our power. Stumbling is not controlled and smooth; it is uncontrolled and unstable. When we stumble, we move forward, but haltingly and erratically and always at risk of falling down.

BRIDGING DIVIDES IN ISRAEL

In 2006, I was happy to be invited to work in Israel. I had been there only once before, briefly, but had felt an unexpected sense of connection. Then when I was in India and needed to locate a synagogue for the Jewish High Holidays, I was surprised that the Israeli Embassy assisted me as if I was one of their own. So when Avner Haramati, a consultant and entrepreneur from Jerusalem, asked me if I would be willing to help him and some of his colleagues organize a national scenario project, I agreed enthusiastically.

The Israeli military had just suffered an unexpected defeat in Lebanon, and Haramati and his colleagues thought there was an opening in Israeli society to rethink where the country was going.[1] "The bitter joke here," he said, "is that, 'If force doesn't work, try more force.' What if that strategy is no longer viable?"

Haramati and his colleagues thought it would be particularly useful to convene a strategic dialogue, not among Israelis and

Palestinians—there were many of these, all stuck—but instead among leaders of different sectors of Jewish Israeli society. Their logic was that until Jewish Israelis could agree among themselves on where they were trying to go, no Jewish Israeli leader would ever have a stable base from which to negotiate a way forward with the Palestinians. One of Haramati's colleagues, Shay Ben Yosef, a consultant and community leader who lived in one of the West Bank settlements, said, "It's always us who is blocking us." So from the beginning this project was, both in its overall framing and for many of the individual participants (including me), richly self-reflective.

Jewish Israeli society is deeply divided and stuck. There are angry and bitter conflicts between religious and secular, left and right, immigrant and native, West Bank settlers and people who live within Israel's pre-1967 armistice lines, and across other cultural, religious, and political fault lines. These deep internal schisms and blockages mirror deep external schisms and blockages, with and among Palestinians and the larger Arab world. In such a fractured social system, people typically try to address their tough challenges by pushing for what they want, regardless of what others want, through some form of aggression.

I once spoke at an Israeli conference of people involved in many kinds of intergroup dialogues: Israeli-Palestinian, Jewish-Arab, religious-secular. I talked with two people who had been involved for years in different dialogues between Jews and Arabs—they said at that time, several hundred such "coexistence" initiatives were under way—and they were deeply discouraged. Steps forward that they had made within particular groups or communities were often reversed by crises in the larger national and international spheres.

I spoke about these challenges to coexistence with Ofer Zalzberg, a political analyst who was a member of our project organizing team. He gave me some insight into the history of such initiatives:

There is a common misunderstanding about what it means for us to engage in a "Track 2" process. Originally "Track 2" referred to informal meetings of top leaders or negotiators who were also involved in formal "Track 1" negotiations. But this crucial ingredient—the involvement in the dialogues of people with real power—has gotten lost, and now people think that any meeting of concerned citizens, influential or not, is a Track 2 process. This is why most of these dialogues produce no results at all.

Later he added further insight into the importance of power:

It is difficult to achieve a sustainable negotiated settlement, through whatever tracks, in a situation that is characterized by asymmetrical power. The stronger party—which in the Israel-Palestine case is Israel—always has the option of enforcing its own solution rather than accepting a mutually agreed solution. You can't make any progress here if you ignore power.

Avner Haramati and his colleagues had years of experience using cross-boundary dialogue to move beyond aggressive war and submissive peace. They invited a diverse cross-section of Jewish Israeli leaders into our project to look for answers to the question, What kind of society can we envisage, to which we and our descendants would be proud to belong and in which we could live together with our non-Jewish neighbors? The innovation in this holistic framing was to re-view the stuck internal questions of Jewish values and vision in the context of the related and fraught external questions. This innovation was mirrored in joint support of the project by Tzav Pius, a Jewish Israeli organization focused on internal cultural-political dialogues, and Oxford Research Group, a British organization focused on international (including Israeli-Arab) peacemaking.

The first workshop was to be held in October 2007. We wanted a setting where the participants would stay for the whole four days and not come and go to other meetings (the largest distance within Israel is only 250 miles). Cyprus is close by and has several significant resonances: it is partly Middle Eastern and partly European; many Jews had been interned there when trying to get to Israel before independence; and it is a popular place for secular Israelis to get married, since within Israel only religious weddings are allowed.

The first workshop almost didn't happen because there were so many heated points of contention among the prospective participants. The different groups of religious participants disagreed on what constituted an acceptable standard for kosher food and on whether a Torah could or should be brought from Israel. Some participants thought it would be morally or religiously incorrect to have such a crucial national conversation on non-Israeli soil; others were reluctant to be so far away from home during a period of elevated security threats. Some left-wing invitees thought it was wrong to have such a conversation without the participation of Israeli Arabs. But in the end, solutions were found to most of these problems, and thirty-one of us met in Cyprus.

The part of the Israeli situation that seemed obvious to me was the manifestation of the two sides of power. On the one hand, I could see in Israelis an impressive and inspiring example of collective power-to: the passionate drive of a people, rising from the ashes of the Holocaust, to realize themselves with increasing intensity (including cultural and religious revival) and extensity (including territorial conquest). Over the sixty years since independence, Israelis had succeeded in co-creating a new social reality. On the other hand, I could see how this drive, set against the analogous and conflicting drive for self-realization of the Palestinians, was producing terribly and reciprocally violent power-over.

Similar power dynamics showed up within our group in Cyprus. All of the participants were seized by a passionate drive to realize themselves: to say what they were thinking, to argue their point of view, to be true to themselves. The culture in the group was democratic and horizontal, and nobody seemed to feel a need to hold back or be deferential. One participant harshly challenged Tova Averbuch, the organizational development consultant who was cofacilitating with Shay Ben Yosef and me, about every aspect of the project plan. Afterwards another participant, seeing that I had been taken aback by the ferocity of the questioning, tried to reassure me: "Don't worry, Israelis are always like this. Even in the Army, we won't follow an order unless the next six steps have also been explained to us." This drive for self-realization, set against the conflicting drives of other participants, created heated and lengthy arguments. Ben Yosef offered an explanation for why workshops in Israel usually aren't placid and conclusive. "Israelis don't like things to be 'tied up neatly with a bow,'" he said. "When we see a package like that, we worry that it might be a bomb."

Working with Avner Haramati, I noticed the primacy he placed on giving everyone the space to exercise their own self-directed power-to. In his roles as both an activist and a consultant, he opposed any attempt to compel or impose change from outside: he believed that change had to come from the inside. In his role as a leader of this project, he fought against any attempt to manipulate or constrain the team's work.

A philosophical and practical pillar of Haramati's way of working is the "Open Space" approach pioneered by Harrison Owen and developed in Israel by Averbuch and Haramati. The only rule of Open Space, says Owen, is "the Law of Two Feet, which says that every individual has two feet, and must be prepared to use them. Individuals can make a difference and must make a difference. If that is not true in a given situation, they, and they alone, must take responsibility to use their two feet, and move to a new place where they can make a difference."² Over the course of the Jewish Israeli Journey project, the participants often used their two feet to move into and out of the project, which therefore swelled and shrank from meeting to meeting.

———

It took me until the team's third workshop—this time held in the southernmost city in Israel, Eilat, beside the Red Sea—to see the manifestation of the complementary dynamic: the two sides of love. One morning the team was having a long and heartfelt dialogue about inclusion and exclusion in Israeli society. To me, every part of the society seemed to feel excluded: the religious, the secular, the settlers, the gays, the Russians, the Arabs. I could hear the pain in participants' voices, but I couldn't make out why this conversation was so important to them.

Suddenly I saw it. The pain in the room arose from a longing for what wasn't there: a sense of inclusion, of connection, of oneness. What I was noticing was the love, the drive towards the unity of the separated, that had motivated the initiating of the project.

The drive towards the unity of the separated in Jewish Israeli society is so strong because the separations are so severe. The increasing conflict both among Jewish Israelis and between them and their neighbors creates increasing physical and social disconnection. In this context, the centrifugal drive of power and the centripetal drive of love are severely in tension.

Within the team, this drive to unity, like the drive to self-realization, was experienced as having two sides. On the one hand, as the work progressed, there was an increasingly relaxed and warm feeling of being a family. This feeling of unity was particularly noticeable during the twenty-four hours of religiously mandated Sabbath rest in the workshops. Instead of working, we relaxed and chatted and talked about the meaning and applicability of the week's Bible reading; these Sabbaths gave our workshops a productive spaciousness (like the Bhavishya team's retreat in the Himalayas). As Rabbi Abraham Joshua Heschel suggests in his book on Jewish spirituality, the Jewish "architecture of holiness" appears not in space but in time. "The Sabbaths," he writes, "are our great cathedrals."[3]

On the other hand, some members of the team felt this drive to familial unity to be stifling. Many of the more universalist, secular members strongly opposed framing the unity of either the team or Israel in exclusive, religious terms.

Underlying many of these conflicts about the right way forward for both the team and the country were disagreements about what constituted the scale and definition of the unity we should pursue. Was it a particular community? All Jewish Israelis? All Israelis, including Palestinian citizens of Israel? Israel and Palestine? All humanity? I thought again about Paul Tillich's definition of love as "the drive towards the unity of the separated." In his book he goes on to say, "Reunion presupposes separation of that which belongs essentially together. Love cannot be described as the union of the strange but as the reunion of the estranged. Estrangement presupposes original oneness."[4] The members of the Israeli team had deeply divergent answers to the fundamental question of what it is that "belongs essentially together" and therefore of what merits unifying action at any particular time.

Knowing that the self-realizing drive of power and the unifying drive of love are always present in every social situation, the challenge is how to notice, reveal, activate, and nurture them, and especially the one that is weaker. Tova Averbuch made a related observation:

> The relationship between power and love reminds me of the figure-ground theory of perception in Gestalt psychology. Often power plays the figure and so is the focus of the people's perception, and love plays the

ground and so is overlooked. By making both of these drives visible and discussable, a facilitator can help a group balance itself.[5]

I talked about these dynamics with Barry Oshry, an organizational development practitioner and theorist, who has for decades studied the behavior of human systems.[6] Oshry has observed four parallel systemic processes: differentiation (the development of a variety of forms and functions), homogenization (the sharing of information and capability), individuation (parts operating separately from one another), and integration (parts connecting into a whole). The power drive, he suggests, involves the processes of differentiation and individuation, and the love drive involves homogenization and integration.[7]

When I looked at the Israeli situation through Oshry's lens, I could see that at many social scales, differentiation and individuation exceeded homogenization and integration. At all of these scales, the fear of being hurt—even of being annihilated—exceeded the fear of hurting others, and so power exceeded love. This phenomenon is accentuated when our ideas are conflated with our identity, so that we take an attack on the former as an attack on the latter. This is a recipe for what U.S. political philosopher John Gardner calls "a war of the parts against the whole."[8] Such imbalances between power and love hobble our attempts to move forward on our tough social challenges.

Israelis are, of course, not the only ones who have been hobbled by a fear of annihilation. In 2004, my colleagues and I facilitated a workshop for the executive team of one of the U.S. government's homeland security agencies. In the aftermath of September 11, they were immersed in foreboding. When I started off one day by asking as I often do what questions the participants were asking themselves, one of them answered, "This morning when I woke up, the question I asked myself was the same one I ask every morning: 'Will New York City be attacked today?'"

At every turn, the workshop conversation ran into this wall of fear and suspicion. One important conversation based on anonymous verbatim quotes from individual interviews with participants about their perspective on their situation ran aground amid suspicion that the reported statements had been made up. A creative dialogue about possible new forms for the organization, sparked by a playful exercise of building models out of sticks and pipe cleaners, was aborted when the agency's CEO, returning to the workshop grim faced from his daily briefing of the president about the day's possible terrorist attacks, suggested that he found the exercise silly. The CEO said about his management philosophy: "A little fear isn't a bad thing," and the final session about how to act on the results of the workshop was cut short when one executive declared deferentially, "We don't need to talk about how we will act; we will simply do what the CEO tells us to do."

I have never been in a workshop where so little moved. Fear rigidifies us and leaves us stuck.

―――――――――――

Through their extended being and working together, the Jewish Israeli project team increased their homogenization and integration. They built a common language—a set of scenarios—for talking about what was happening and might happen in and around Israel. They built relationships among themselves that served as bridges across the chasms that separated their communities. Averbuch gives an example of this bridging that resembles the moment of communion in Guatemala:

f hy being other

In one of our later meetings, Rabbi Azriel Azriel, from the Council of the Rabbis of the Settlements, was reflecting on how fundamentally his perspective had shifted through our working together. He said, "What I now see, and what surprises me, is that I would rather live in a scenario that I didn't choose and do not like but that takes me and my needs into consideration, than in a scenario that I do like but that does not take you into consideration." After he said that, the room fell into a sacred silence—and Israelis are not often silent. This was one of those precious moments of grace that makes worthwhile all of the trials and tribulations of our journey.⁹

This increased homogenization and integration and hence increased balance of the team's drives enabled them to discuss previously undiscussable realities and to create new options. New social realities within the team opened up possibilities for new social realities in the larger system. This was especially true of innovative political and diplomatic options for depolarizing the conflicts over Jewish versus Palestinian sovereignty and identity. Subsequent to the scenario workshops, many members of the team became better known and more senior and influential within their own organizations and communities, and so these realities and options also became better known and more seriously discussed within Jewish Israeli society, with Diaspora Jews, and between Israelis and Palestinians. In these ways, the work of the team is contributing to rebalancing these interconnected social systems and thereby helping them to advance.

The team had no illusions about the extent of their contribution or influence. The oldest member of the team was Rabbi Shlomo Pappenheim, a leader in the ultra-Orthodox community. He reminded us of the admonition in the Jewish *Ethics of the Fathers*: "It is not up to you to complete the work, but neither are you at liberty to desist from it." The team did not desist, but neither have they completed what needs to be done.

———

Right after the Jewish Israeli team's third workshop in Eilat, I flew to Oman to give a speech at the biennial global meeting of the Society for Organizational Learning. I had been a member of the SoL community for years, and we were excited to meet for the first time in a Muslim country; the title of the meeting was "Bridging the Gulf." I expected that this encounter might be charged, because within the meeting's organizing committee there had been months of anxiety about whether and how many Israeli members of SoL would be granted visas for Oman. At the last minute only Avner Haramati and another Israeli member of the committee got visas, and they decided not to attend. There was one Israeli at the meeting, a man who held dual nationality, but he was afraid and wasn't letting anyone know where he was from. I could feel the tension in my stomach.

I gave my speech about power and love, using as one of my examples my two sets of two-sided experiences in Israel. This provoked an angry response from many people in the audience. One Palestinian man stood up and complained that my talk had been unbalanced in its empathetic interpretation of the Israeli situation. I was nervous, but thought this argument was healthy because part of the reality of the gulfs between us was now being discussed.

But then the chair of the session cut off the argument and moved us into a break. I was scheduled to be on the meeting's closing panel at the end of the day, but now I was too controversial and was removed.

In this meeting in Oman I saw the opposite dynamic from the one I had seen in the Israeli meetings. In Oman the fear of offending or hurting others (including the conference hosts and sponsors), of shattering the fragile unity of the group, dominated. Love exceeded power. This left the SoL members—like the Israeli team had been at first—constrained in moving forward on the challenges they wanted to address.

BUILDING DEMOCRACY IN SOUTH AFRICA

In 2008, fifteen years after I had moved from London to Cape Town, I was given an opportunity to reengage in earnest with South Africa, my adopted country. Bob Head, an executive of Old Mutual, contacted me. Old Mutual owns the country's biggest group of financial services companies, and in 1991 it had sponsored a national scenario project to which Mont Fleur had been the antiestablishment reply. Now Bob Head and his colleagues, hopeful and fearful about what they saw happening in the country, thought it would again be useful to convene an independent dialogue among South African leaders—politicians from all parties, businesspeople, activists, academics—about possible futures for the country, and they asked me to lead the design and facilitation of the exercise. We called the project Dinokeng (*Dinokeng* is a Sepedi word meaning "place of rivers"), after the name of the location of our workshops and because the work brought together different streams of national thought and action.[10]

The South Africa I came back to in 2008, after years working elsewhere in the world, was chaotic, conflictual, and confusing. The African National Congress, the party that had been in power since the election of Nelson Mandela in 1994, was roiling with factional battles that were spilling over into many parts of the government and into the courts. The economy had boomed and was now slumping, in part because of power shortages. Education, health, and security conditions were deteriorating. More than sixty people were killed in a wave of xenophobic attacks. Dinokeng reimmersed me in this tumultuous and bewildering mess.

If in 1993 I had fallen in love with South Africa, now, fifteen years later, I fell out of love. Psychologist Robert Johnson argues that, unlike other-centered uniting love, romantic "falling in love" is ultimately self-centered: "Romance must, by its very nature, deteriorate into egotism. The passion of romance is always directed at our own projections, our own expectations, our own fantasies."[11] I became disillusioned, which is to say that I could see through my own illusions and projections and fantasies, and therefore see more clearly what was going on in the country.

Right after I got back to South Africa, I attended a meeting with Israeli psychologist Shlomo Breznitz. He drew a parallel between the disillusionment that I and many South Africans were experiencing and what the Israelis, sixty years after their independence, felt when they looked back on their earlier idealistic belief that everything was possible. In order to maintain hope, he said, we need to believe that the future can be better than the present and to see milestones of progress. But whereas the milestones of independence or democracy are clear, progress on complex challenges such as poverty or reconciliation comes only slowly and with many ups and downs. This makes it hard to maintain hope and forward movement.

In this complex and less hopeful context, I found the Dinokeng exercise challenging to lead. My colleague Kees van der Heijden had once pointed out to me that group processes are vulnerable to two opposite pitfalls: on one side is excessive homogeneity, or groupthink, in which everyone agrees (love without enough power) and so fail to see when their agreement is in error. On the other side is excessive differentiation, or fragmentation, in which everyone has a different perspective (power without enough love) and so can't move forward together.[12] In Dinokeng, we kept stumbling between these two extremes.

I saw and felt this stumbling most clearly in the third workshop, when we were trying to agree on our scenarios and conclusions. When the meeting started, on a Thursday evening, the team expressed great pessimism. They weren't happy with the progress we had made in our previous workshops, and they doubted whether by the planned end of this meeting on Sunday, we could achieve our objective. I too was worried, but when I got back to my room after this session, I realized that I could not control whether the team succeeded or failed. What I needed to do was to let go of my worry (which in Bhavishya I had felt unable to do) and open up to what the team could co-create.

I spent most of Friday wrestling with the team. Lots of people had lots to say, and I thought if I didn't keep a tight rein on the agenda, we would never make progress. During a break, one of the project's conveners took me aside and suggested that I loosen up the agenda a bit and give the people who wanted to talk more opportunity to do so. I did this, and by Saturday afternoon, to my surprise, the people who wanted to had said their piece and then relaxed and also let go.

But by now we were way behind schedule, and I didn't see how we could complete our work on time. I put this question about the rest of the meeting's agenda to the team as a whole, and they quickly and easily decided, first, how to adjust the work plan and, second, to start early on Sunday morning. By the time the meeting ended at lunch on Sunday, we had—contrary to everyone's expectations, including mine—finished our work well.

The team and I stumbled between power and love, and we moved forward. At first I emphasized unity—staying on the team's task and agenda—but the people who wanted to express themselves felt constrained and manipulated, and they pushed back. But this extended period of individual self-realization put the team at risk of failing to achieve their collective task, and they pulled themselves together and ahead.

The team's forward movement produced a creative break-through. They agreed on three possible scenarios for South Africa: "Walk Apart," a story of continued social disintegra-tion and decay; "Walk Behind," of an interventionist and

paternalistic state; and "Walk Together," of an enabling state and an engaged citizenry. The team's primary conclusion was that a positive future for the country depended on citizens and leaders from all sectors (not just the government) reengaging actively and robustly with the country's tough social challenges—as many had done during the pre-1994 struggle against apartheid, but as most had not after the election of a democratic government. The team's insight was that forward movement for the country required people to wade into the battles involved in reconnecting their own self-realizing to the nation's self-realizing.

When we ended the meeting on Sunday, the team's final round of comments indicated that they themselves had, through these workshops, shifted in precisely the way they were now urging on their compatriots. They had seen how they were part of the problem ("since 1994, we have messed up," said one) and therefore how they could be part of the solution. "I arrived stuck," one team member said, "but now, through being with others, I am unstuck; I had lost my voice, but now I have found it." Others said: "I now see opportunity and possibility and also my responsibility." "We were angry and felt unwanted, alienated, despairing, lonely, and victimized; now we feel more open, committed, compassionate, and hopeful." "You're all talking of *re*-engaging: I never was engaged but now I am." The Dinokeng team members were happy because they could now see how to fully engage their energies in the service of the country to which they essentially belonged. Their communion strengthened their agency and vice versa. This recommitment to national service inspired me, and over the months that followed, it inspired many South Africans.

My partner Zaid Hassan suggests that two conditions are necessary for a team to be healthy:

> A group displays collective intelligence when the conditions of diversity in its composition and access to information by its members are met. If a group lacks diversity or lacks information, then it will in all likelihood not display signs of collective intelligence, but rather will tend to either conflict or groupthink. Groups that are able to meet conditions for collective intelligence will be able to make decisions in complex social systems that may well appear messy or illogical in the short-term, but will ultimately result in systems that are more resilient and hence sustainable.[13]

The Dinokeng team met these two conditions and so exhibited collective intelligence and contributed to the resilience and sustainability of South Africa.

Zaid goes on to say that, in order to meet these conditions, a team needs a "container."[14] He quotes Crane Stookey, founder of The Nova Scotia Sea School: "The container is any closed, inescapable environment. It can be 12 people in a 28 foot open boat for 3 weeks at the Sea School, or it can be the river, the ropes course, even the workplace. The image that best describes this principle is the stone polisher, the can that turns and tumbles the rocks we found at the beach until they turn into gems. The rocks don't get out until they're done, the friction between them, the chaos of their movement, is what polishes them, and in the end the process reveals their natural inherent brilliance. We don't paint colors on them, we trust what's there."[15]

Gabrielle Rifkind is a group analyst who directs the Oxford Research Group's Human Security in the Middle East programme and who was a member of the organizing team of the Jewish Israeli project. She also highlights the importance of carefully constructing a container:

> The positioning of the group facilitator is complex. We can never get people to go where they don't want to go, but we can name the tensions, the complexities, and the struggles, and thereby allow more mature decision making by the group. We do not just create the space for the self-expression of a group: a frame exists to remind us why we are there. This frame or container is held by the facilitator or conductor in the group. In group analytic terms, those conducting the group take an enormous amount of care in the construction of the group, who is in it, and what the parameters are. There are always limitations and restrictions in any space, psychological or political, and operating within this space becomes an opportunity to test the relationship between power and love and how they co-exist.[16]

The Dinokeng team had a strong container because of the deliberate way in which we had set up the project. The purpose of the exercise was clear and shared; its conveners (six eminent persons, five of them independent of the sponsors) were legitimate and engaged; the team's ground rules and ways of working were carefully formulated and agreed; the workshop venue was private and peaceful; the project was well resourced and staffed; and the team took the time to build up their relationships with one another. Within this container, the team had the capacity, not always to stay on track, but to correct themselves when they got too far off track. The team went down many blind alleys, but always managed to backtrack and move forward again. In such co-creative work, missteps are unavoidable; what is important is not to avoid mistakes but to avoid nonmovement.

I cofacilitated the Dinokeng workshops with Ishmael Mkhabela, a South African community organizer who helps poor people empower themselves to improve their lives. Mkhabela manages the dilemma of power and love skillfully. He focuses on connecting to the context, priorities, and will of the people he is organizing. He invests in building a friendly and accountable relationship, within which he and they can talk openly about what really matters to each of them. He knows that such enduring human connections are essential. Once, upset with the inconsiderate way some members of the Dinokeng team were acting, he exclaimed, "It seems to me that some of you have no expectations of a relationship beyond this project!" Another time he said to me, "Recognition means the acceptance of the other and their interests and values, even if they are opposite to yours. Our job is not to preach to or convert them, but to be comfortable in the same space. We cannot all jump into one seat, but we all want to sit down."

But Mkhabela's role as an organizer is not simply as a coach or friend. He is not only helping people get where they want to go; he has his own intentionality. He is trying to effect a certain social change, and he knows that to do this he must engage not only people's humanity but also his and their power and interests. He once said to me about Dinokeng, "The members of our team are not nuns, they are not priests; they have not taken vows not to have interests. People's interests are not the problem; it is only a problem when those of one overpower those of others." Mkhabela's approach to co-creating new social realities is to build and unite the power of multiple actors, so that they can realize both their own potentials and the larger potential of the system of which they are a part.

Mkhabela used to work with Edward Chambers, the successor of legendary community organizer Saul Alinsky at the Industrial Areas Foundation in Chicago (Barack Obama worked there before he went to Harvard Law School). Chambers believes that community leaders can, through relationship, expand their power-to:

> People who can understand the concerns of others and mix those concerns with their own agenda have access to a power source denied to those who can push only their own interests. In this fuller understanding, "power" is a verb meaning "to give and take," "to be reciprocal," "to be influenced as well as to influence." To be affected by another in relationship is as true a sign of power as the capacity to affect others. Rela tional power is infinite and unifying, not limited and divisive. It's additive and multiplicative, not subtractive and divisive. As you become more powerful, so do those in relationship with you. As they become more powerful, so do you. This is power understood as relational, as power with, not *over*.[17]

Chambers also believes that power and love are complementary:

> In Western culture, "power" means "unilateral power" and "love" means "unilateral love." So Westerners tend to see power and love as opposites, and the right relationship between them as a kind of balancing off of the effects of these two ways of relating. When we "power" someone, we ignore their interests; when we "love" someone, we ignore our own concerns. Power and love—like self-interest and self-sacrifice—are not, however, mutually exclusive, but are rather complementary aspects of a conjugal partnership. There can be no creative power without some acknowledgment of the other's interests, just as there can be no healthy love if the self is wholly lost in concern for the other. Power and love are two-way streets.[18]

The community organizing approach to effecting social change in this way works with power and love so that each strengthens the other.

The experience of working on the Dinokeng project gave me an opportunity to reflect not just on the microdynamics of this team but also on the macrodynamics of the country. When I looked back on the previous decades of South African history, an underlying trend I could make out was an exhilarating and terrifying roller-coaster ride between power and love.

In 1993, when I emigrated from London to Cape Town, South Africa was at the peak of its drive towards the unity of the separated. Three years earlier, the white minority government of F. W. de Klerk had released the erstwhile "terrorist" Nelson Mandela from prison and legalized the African National Congress and the other opposition parties. The years that followed saw an intense series of on-again-off-again negotiations—large and small, national and local, open and secret—among these and other stakeholders. The Mont Fleur Scenario Exercise was one of these many parallel efforts, all of them aimed at agreeing on how to effect the transition away from apartheid's rigid political, economic, and social separation. In 1994, these negotiations succeeded in producing a settlement on an interim constitution and on democratic elections, in which Nelson Mandela became president.

President Mandela epitomized and emphasized this drive towards unity. He took many actions intended to symbolize and effect this reconciliation. Just before the Rugby World Cup match began in Johannesburg in 1995, Mandela walked out onto the field wearing a jersey with the name and number of François Pienaar, the South African team's Afrikaner captain. Rugby, more than any other sport in South Africa, is identified with Afrikaners, the whites who spearheaded the creation of the apartheid system. Journalist John Carlin, in his book about this defining moment in the South African transition, quotes Morné du Plessis, the Afrikaner manager of the team: "I walked out into this bright, harsh winter sunlight and at first I could not make out what was going on, what the people were chanting, why there was so much excitement before the players had even gone out onto the field. Then I made out the words. This crowd of white people, of Afrikaners, as one man, as one nation, they were chanting, 'Nel-son! Nel-son! Nel-son.'... I don't think I'll ever experience a moment like that again. It was a moment of magic, a moment of wonder. It was the moment I realized that there really was a chance this country could work."[19]

Apartheid (this Afrikaans word means "apartness") had been based on the doctrine that each racial and ethnic group belonged essentially together and needed to be separated from the others. Apartheid was a set of rules governing where each different group was allowed to live and work, whom they were allowed to marry, and of which "country" they were allowed to be citizens (the black homelands were recognized only by the South African government). Mandela succeeded in leading South Africans to enlarge their definition of what it was that belonged essentially together.

In 1993, one week after I immigrated to South Africa, Chris Hani, the popular black president of the South African Communist Party, was assassinated outside his home in Johannesburg by a right-wing white immigrant. The assassin was quickly arrested, in part because one of Hani's neighbors, an Afrikaner woman, had written down his license plate number. We were all afraid that this act would precipitate a bloody uprising, and then-President de Klerk asked Mandela to go on national television to appeal for calm. Mandela said, "A white man, full of prejudice and hate, came to our country and committed a deed so foul that our whole nation teeters on the brink of disaster. A white woman, of Afrikaner origin, risked her life so that we may know, and bring to justice, this assassin."[20] Mandela succeeded in reframing the situation away from "black versus white" to "all South Africans together versus those who attack us."

In South Africa, I facilitated many multi-stakeholder social change projects. South Africa was an extraordinary place to do this kind of work because so much needed to be done and so many committed and competent people were engaged in doing it. The essence of what we were all trying to do was expressed perfectly by the phrase used in Afrikaans for "affirmative action": *regstellende aksie*, which literally means "right-putting action." Right-putting action means purposeful action to realize the wholeness of a social system. To live in South Africa is to be immersed in both the need and the energy for right-putting action.

Between 1993 and 1995, I worked on many such projects, dealing with education, energy, policing, economics, mining, and politics, and involving leaders from government, business, and civil society. But by 1996, the emphasis placed on such cross-sector efforts was diminishing. These same challenges were being addressed, but now with more emphasis on work within rather than across institutions. The new government, now legitimately elected, wanted to get on with governing. The newly appointed civil servants wanted to focus on getting their departments working properly and in line with the new government's political priorities. Business executives wanted to focus on growing their companies in the now much more open and competitive national and international markets. The emphasis had again swung from love back to power.

I noticed analogous shifts in individuals. Activists who for decades had sacrificed their careers and families and bank balances and lives for "the struggle" now wanted to sacrifice less and realize themselves more. The unity within political organizations that had been maintained during the struggle now diminished in the face of self-realizing "careerism" and "factionalism." Interracial tensions increased. Blacks thought Mandela had been too conciliatory towards whites, who, in spite of the new political dispensation, expected to maintain their economic and social privileges. Whites thought they and their children were being squeezed out of the country's future. Ethnic and religious groups became more confident in asserting their separate identities. As this attention to self-realization increased, the patience and space for unity decreased.

By the beginning of 2007, this fragmentation and polarization reached a breaking point. Several top public figures were charged with extremely self-realizing corruption. The African National Congress had a tumultuous party conference in which many of its incumbent leaders—including Thabo Mbeki, the president of both the party and the country—were deposed. Many people were frightened of the growing conflict and chaos and were losing faith in the capacity of the government, the ruling party, and the society as a whole to maintain safety and unity. Talk of emigration—of abandoning the national unity—surged.

But then by mid-2008, a renewed drive to unity emerged. More and more people stepped forward—in speeches and conferences and civil society initiatives of all sorts—to express their concern about these fragmenting trends and to bring people together to address them. Dinokeng was one prominent manifestation of this drive. The prevailing view in these initiatives was that the increasingly robust intellectual, political, and legal contestations were signs of vitality, signs that people who in various ways had been marginalized and suppressed were now finding their voice and asserting themselves. At the same time, these powerful assertions had to be prevented from tearing the country apart.

As I came to notice this national rhythm of dangerous and creative stumbling between power and love, I came to understand the critical importance of a national "container." What kind of container could prevent a falling-down disconnection between power and love? What kind of container could, when self-realizing goes too far and creates a war of the parts against the whole, call forth corrective unifying and, when unifying goes too far and creates stasis, call forth corrective self-realizing? What kind of container could enable the country to be resilient and healthy?

Finally I understood why so many South Africans, including the members of the Dinokeng team, place so much importance on the robustness of the nation's vision and values and especially on the codification of these in the carefully negotiated constitution and judicial system. These ideas and institutions provide the container—the checks and balances—that prevents both individualistic self-realizing power and collective unifying love from going too far. If these ideas and institutions weaken, society weakens.

How to stumble

We often stumble because often one of our drives is stronger or more relied upon than the other. In some places and times, the drive that we emphasize is power—for example, in many business and political contexts and in periods of conflict. In other places and times, it is love—for example, in many community and spiritual contexts and in periods of communion.

What must we do when we find ourselves stumbling and thus impaired in our capacity to co-create new social realities? We must build up or bring in our weaker drive.

When our power dominates, we must pay attention to and strengthen our love. In the context of a multiactor initiative to address a tough social challenge, this means emphasizing processes for social homogenization and integration. These include dialogic processes such as meetings or encounters or workshops that bring together and connect separated actors and help them see their shared situation more empathetically and holistically.

When our love dominates, we must pay attention to and strengthen our power. This means emphasizing processes for social differentiation and individuation. These include activist and entrepreneurial processes that empower actors to recognize, choose, and act on their own course of self-realization. (Zoughbi Zoughbi, the Palestinian activist and facilitator who in 2005 warned me of the danger of ignoring power, also shared

with me his recipe for righting power imbalances: "Strengthen the weak and bring the strong to their senses.")

When in these ways we employ more of both our power and our love, each builds the other and makes it stronger and more generative.

In addition to employing these processes for strengthening our weaker drive, we must also pay attention to processes for bringing into play our already strong but underemployed drive. These rebalancing processes include focusing on feedback, regulatory, and governance processes and containers that help us notice where we are and correct ourselves accordingly.

Stumbling is dangerous but also healthy. To be healthy does not mean that we never fall ill. It means that when we do fall ill or out of balance—physically, mentally, spiritually—we have the capacity to heal and rebalance ourselves.[21]

Often stumbling is as good as it gets. Stumbling is more advanced than falling, and walking is harder to achieve. It is worth understanding and learning how to stumble.

6
Walking

*W*HEN WE WALK, we employ rhythmically first one leg and then the other. When we walk, we engage both our power and our love, each balancing out and bringing in and building up the other. When we walk, we move forward, learning as we go.

GROWING SUSTAINABLE FOOD IN EUROPE AND THE AMERICAS

Hal Hamilton is a farmer, activist, and researcher who has worked for decades on the economic, environmental, and social challenges involved in producing food. When we first met in 2002, he explained to me why food production—the largest industry in the world, one on which every person in the world depends—cannot be sustained in its current form. Food production has kept up with the population growth over the past decades (through the use of a lot of fossil fuel–based fertilizers), but it has done so in a way that delivers inexpensive food to rich people and expensive food to poor people, leaving one billion people undernourished. It uses half of the earth's habitable land and three-quarters of its fresh water, has decimated many fisheries, and has degraded continent-sized expanses of soil.

This at-risk system epitomizes our interconnection and interdependence with each other and with the earth. Indian

103

environmentalist Vandana Shiva writes, "Despite our diversity and differences, we are all connected: connected through the earth, our mother; connected through food, the very web of life; connected through our common humanity, which makes a peasant the equal of a prince."[1]

I recognized in these descriptions of the global food system a situation characterized by high fullness and high dynamic, social, and generative complexity. Hal Hamilton and I thought that together we could develop a project that was systemic, participative, and emergent enough to meet this complexity and to contribute to addressing these interrelated challenges.

We started to talk with people we knew and others whom they knew. We discovered that there were leaders in many parts of the system—from food companies, farmer organizations, and environmental and social NGOs—who from different starting points had reached the same conclusion: the mainstream system is unsustainable, and what they were doing on their own was not having a significant impact on making it more sustainable. Out of these conversations, Hamilton and I decided to try to create an alliance of these leaders "to accelerate the shift of sustainability in the food system from niche to mainstream." Our objective was to co-create "living examples" of sustainable food supply chains that we, and others whom we might influence and inspire, could grow into a more sustainable mainstream food system.

It took us a year to find and recruit the initial members of what became known as the Sustainable Food Lab.[2] The people who joined us cared about these issues, were entrepreneurial and action oriented, and had reached the limit of what they could do alone and so were eager to enter into new partnerships. Later, a senior executive of SYSCO, the largest food distributor in the United States, said, "It's pretty unusual for fierce competitors like SYSCO and U.S. Foodservice to come together and work for the higher good. The essence, the power, of the Sustainable Food Lab is that we can do 100-fold, 1000-fold, more together than we can do by ourselves. What we're doing is the right thing to do, the good thing to do—for the world. It's also good for our businesses."[3] Other people who also cared about these issues decided not to join us because they believed they could better realize their objectives outside such partnerships: a corporate executive who wanted to pursue his own commercial opportunities, a farmer activist who wanted to mobilize protests against mainstream organizations, a government leader who wanted to let others propose policies that he could review at arm's length.

The lab team consisted of forty-five leaders from governments, food processors, retailers, banks, nongovernmental organizations, and citizen and worker movements, from across Europe, the United States, and Latin America. We met for the first time in June 2004 in Bergen in the Netherlands. The hotel where we met had previously housed a Folk High School, part of a pre-World War II Danish movement to create antifascist "free islands": extended courses for workers, farmers, intellectuals, and unemployed people that included lectures, working in the fields, and poetry and music. Our intention was, likewise, to engage the lab team's heads, hearts, and hands.

The first part of this work was co-sensing: immersing ourselves together in the complexity of our current and emerging reality. This required us to venture beyond the comfortable boundaries of our everyday world—our habitual places and relationships and thoughts—to see afresh what was happening and was possible. In Bergen we had a team that constituted a microcosm of the social system involved in food. As members talked with one another openly, the whole group saw more of the whole system, from multiple perspectives, in all its complexities and contradictions. At the end of that meeting, one participant said, "I was surprised by the fact that after two and a half days, some sort of shared understanding has emerged despite us coming from very, very different backgrounds. I think part of the reason for this is that there has been among the team a very high level of willingness to learn and listen to other people."[4]

Three months after Bergen, the lab team continued this co-sensing by going on "learning journeys." In three groups of fifteen, we made weeklong trips to three different parts of Brazil, where many aspects of the global food system—production and consumption, rural and urban, traditional and modern, sustainable and unsustainable—were manifested locally. I led a group that visited peasants, retailers, industry spokespersons, large-scale growers, consumer research organizations, and government departments. Through these encounters, we built up a shared picture of the food system and how it worked and why it was producing the results it was producing. I had been delighted with our kickoff meeting in Bergen and had thought that the lab team had connected and learned a lot there. But later, one of the team members told me that it had only been in Brazil—with its long bus rides and meals and late-night chats—that the team had really opened themselves and their thinking.

In November 2004, the lab team met again, this time in rural Arizona, for the co-presencing part of our process. As the members of this committed, influential, microcosmic team immersed themselves more and more deeply in the reality of the system they were trying to understand and change, they began to notice their own role in things being the way they are and to imagine their own role in things becoming better. When they then retreated from the complexity of that system and reflected on what was going on around and within themselves, they were able to see what role they could play and therefore what they had to do next.

We started this meeting by sharing stories from our three learning journeys. Then we left the hotel and were guided into the nearby desert, where we were to spend seventy-two hours in individual campsites out of sight of one another. We did not have any particular assignment for this time: just to step back from the noise of our situation, quiet ourselves down, open up, and see what we could see.

The campsites were near the U.S.-Mexico border, and in the middle of the second night, we were all woken up by the ferocious sound of a big black helicopter that the Immigration and Naturalization Service was using to hunt people trying to cross the border illegally into the United States. This unexpected disturbance was shocking to everyone in our group, but produced two different reactions. Most of the white Americans and Europeans went back to sleep, unfazed, even reassured by the police presence. But most of the Latin Americans, empathizing with the hunted Hispanic border crossers, were terrified or enraged. One of them later pointed out that many of these immigrants were heading north because the rural food-producing economies from which they came could no longer support them. So one of the differences and dynamics most central to the work we were doing had made a dramatic appearance in the middle of our retreat.

At the end of the three days, we gathered to share our experiences. For some of us, the retreat was a time of relaxed, curious observation, and for others, of intense, even disturbing soul searching. Susan Sweitzer, the project learning historian, notes that "many team members commented on the sense of calm determination in the group after the wilderness camping experience and expressed confidence that this group was uniquely capable of the work that was needed in the food system. Others remarked on a feeling of good-heartedness and convergence. Many became aware of a new level of commitment and energy."[5]

Everything that had happened up to this point in the meeting—our reflections on seeing the whole food system in microcosm in Bergen and Brazil, our insights from the desert—had primed the lab team to answer the question, What is needed of us?

Back at the hotel, we were ready to talk about how to answer this question and so to move forward with our Food Lab work. The session started with members announcing the ideas they had energy to work on. Using the Open Space approach (the approach I later learned more about in Israel), they quickly formed groups around these ideas; these groups evolved into initiatives that the lab team worked on over the years that followed. I had used this Open Space approach many times, but had never before seen a team organize themselves with such alacrity and enthusiasm. It was as if their months of co-sensing and co-presencing activities had produced a common understanding out of which their ideas and energies naturally flowed.

One of our guests at this meeting was Brian Arthur, the economist at the Santa Fe Institute whom Joseph Jaworski and Otto Scharmer had interviewed in their research on the U-Process. He had been on many solo retreats, and he spoke to the team about his own experiences and understanding of the value of retreating—of stepping back from intense engagement with a complex problem you are trying to solve—for breakthrough innovation. When Arthur observed the lab team just before the Open Space, he said, "They are both completely still and completely ready to act."

At the time, Arthur was writing a book about technological innovation. His thesis was that new technologies arise through new and unexpected combinations of existing ones.[6] The initiatives that the lab team chose after their retreat were not new: the members and others had thought of and talked about these ideas before. What was new was the combination of ideas and actors present in a common space and animated by a common intention.

The potential of the Food Lab to create innovations to shift global food systems arose primarily from this potential to create new, trusting connections among leading actors. "Social innovation arises not only from new ideas," says Angela Wilkinson of the University of Oxford, "but from new networks of relationships."[7] Mari Fitzduff, who for decades played an important facilitating role in the peace process in Northern Ireland, once made a similar remark: "In these situations, the solution is rarely the problem. The solution to the Northern Ireland conflict had been sitting for many years in a filing cabinet. What was needed, and what eventually occurred, was for the protagonists to go together to the filing cabinet."[8] The space that the Food Lab provided enabled its members to act more wisely because they had a greater view of the whole. Their love redirected their power.

The members of the lab team were moved by this increasingly dense set of connections. In the closing of the Arizona meeting, one of the businessmen said, "I have heard others in the circle call it 'trust' and 'respect,' but I've just got to say, I have experienced a deepening love for all of you."[9] Through their experiences together, in meetings, on learning journeys, and in the desert, they now knew one another better and related to one another both as colleagues and as friends. Although they had different backgrounds and loyalties and positions in the larger system, they saw one another as peers in a common enterprise. For some of them, their sense of their own identity was shifting. They were excited by what they could sense was the enlarging potential within and among themselves.

During the time we were on our desert retreat, some Native Americans were on an adjacent piece of land, undertaking a similar process in their own tradition: a vision quest. Afterwards, some of us participated with them in a ceremonial sweat lodge. The leader of the ceremony kept intoning the ritual phrase, "All my relations." Arizona reminded us of our connections and kinship with one another and with all life.

In April 2005, five months later, we came together again in a big country house outside Salzburg, Austria. The purpose of this meeting was to translate the team's general shared understandings of the food system, and of initiatives they might undertake to make it more sustainable, into concrete agreements to build joint pilot projects.

What struck me in Salzburg was how much more tension and conflict there was than there had been during the team's previous meetings. My colleague Alain Wouters noticed this too and said to me, "What we are seeing here is the natural characteristic of the team having shifted into action. Now for the first time their interests and power are truly engaged: who will deploy their time and resources on what, who will have what control and ownership of what we produce, and who will get the credit or blame." This shift into co-realizing brought with it a distinctly different energy and way of working.

Co-realizing is the process of growing new social realities from the ground up. It means working with our hands and with partners—not just on paper or on our own—to learn what works, not only in theory but in practice. Trevor Manuel, a member of the South African Mont Fleur team who had afterwards become that country's minister of finance and then of planning, explained why this approach is necessary in situations of high complexity, such as the one his team had faced: "There was a high degree of flux at that time: there was no paradigm. There was no precedent, there was nothing. So we had to carve it."[10] Co-realizing is a process of collective, hands-on carving of new social realities.

Over the five years since its launch, the Food Lab has contributed to building and has grown to be an important player in the now much stronger global food sustainability movement. The lab has a growing number of members and projects, and it is involved in initiatives not only in Europe and the Americas, but also in Africa and Asia. Its activities have become focused on the practical work of learning how to improve particular value chains—work that by definition involves uniting the separated across organizations, sectors, and countries. Out of these learnings, a new, more sustainable approach to managing food systems, embodied in shared models, measurements, and standards, is growing. Hal Hamilton describes it this way:

The Sustainable Food Lab is now far enough along, and its members influential enough, to measure project results in large numbers: hundreds of millions of dollars, millions of acres, tens of thousands of people. These results are important but can be distracting. The world is littered with success stories with "measurable outputs" that don't add up to systemic change. The role of the Lab is to connect these leaders to one another, to support them in their organizational and project roles, and to nurture the shared space in which they grow in their capacities to lead the whole system.[11]

Peter Senge has been involved in the Food Lab since its inception. He calls it "the largest and most promising systemic change initiative I know of."[12] In his book *The Dance of Change*, Senge writes, "Most leadership strategies are doomed to failure from the outset. Leaders instigating change are often like gardeners standing over their plants, imploring them: 'Grow! Try harder! You can do it!' No gardener tries to convince a plant to 'want' to grow: if the seed does not have the potential to grow, there's nothing anyone can do to make a difference."[13]

The members of the Food Lab have been good gardeners. They have nurtured rather than implored their plants. Their approach has been to create seed initiatives that have the potential to bear fruit and produce more seeds and eventually grow into a more sustainable mainstream food system. Many seeds don't sprout, and some of the Food Lab's initiatives have died while others have been weeded out. But some have taken root and are being cultivated and, although still fragile, are growing bigger and stronger. Team members have focused their energies less on opposing the efforts of others and more on removing obstacles to the self-realizing growth of those of their own initiatives that have life. Here they are employing designer Buckminster Fuller's admonition: "You never change things by fighting existing

reality. To change something, build a new model that makes the existing model obsolete."[14]

When I went to Brazil for the Food Lab learning journey, I met with Helio Mattar, the president of a nongovernmental organization named Akatu, which works with companies to promote "conscious consumption." *Akatu* in the indigenous Brazilian Tupi language means both "seed" and "world." Mattar believes that a better world is contained and can be generated from the seeds of changes in the consciousness and actions of individuals. The Food Lab is a promising example of this approach.

MITIGATING CLIMATE CHANGE IN CANADA

In 2007, I got involved in another set of efforts aimed at addressing a sustainability-related challenge: climate change. This work brought me back full circle to the beginning of my work on complex challenges—and now these challenges looked different. When I had entered graduate school in 1982, I had switched my studies from natural sciences to social sciences in order to work on global energy and environmental problems, and when I had joined Shell in 1988, the first set of scenarios I had worked on posited these problems being solved through a systemic transition to low-carbon fuels. But the twenty-plus years since then taught me that tough social challenges are not simply problems that can be solved like those in a physics textbook. As my colleague Kees van der Heijden taught, they are instead "problematic situations"—situations that different actors understand and view as problematic in different ways—that can be worked on and through but that keep evolving and never get "fixed." The best we can do is to walk forward, with others, and through such walking, co-create new possibilities and new realities.

My reimmersion in the problematic climate change situation came through a series of conversations that climatologist Earl Saxon and I held over several months with thirty-five international climate researchers and negotiators. We were trying to understand whether and how a multi-stakeholder process like the Sustainable Food Lab might be helpful in shifting this most complex, vital, urgent, and difficult challenge.

I understood from these conversations that climate change epitomizes, in the extreme, everything we know about tough social challenges: how they arise, why we get stuck, and what it takes to get unstuck and to move forward. It demonstrates the extreme fullness of our world and the global interdependence this produces. It exemplifies extreme dynamic, social, and generative complexity: cause and effect interlinked and separated by decades and continents; deeply differing perspectives and priorities among the worldwide actors involved; and a situation that no one has ever faced before. And it provides an extreme answer to the question of what it is that belongs essentially together and that is therefore driven to reunification: all of humanity, plus the ecosystems on which we depend.

Climate change demands that we co-create new low-carbon social realities on a scale and at a speed that is without precedent. It demands that we learn how collectively to exercise 100 percent of our power and 100 percent of our love.

The dominant ways that humanity is currently acting in relation to climate are the extreme, polarized, degenerative ones: aggressive war and submissive peace. We burn fossil fuels to provide ourselves with power-to, literally, but we do this in denial of the impacts of our activities on climate and on other people. Earl Saxon says about the futility of denying our interconnectedness: "Mother Nature does not negotiate."[15]

The central forum for making international agreements to reduce the global emissions of greenhouse gases is the United Nations Framework Convention on Climate Change (UNFCCC). In these negotiations, almost all of the participating national governments focus not on the shared imperative to mitigate climate change but on protecting their divergent national interests. To avoid the worst impacts of climate change, global emissions would need to be decreased by 50 percent of their 1990 levels by 2050 (perhaps by much more), but because of this relentlessly disconnected power-to, after fifteen-plus years of UNFCCC negotiations, emissions have actually *increased*. This unmitigated climate change will impose widespread starvation and migration—as if from a war—on those least able to cope. By denying our interconnectedness, our local power-to has morphed into global power-over.

Binding agreements in the UNFCCC require the unanimous consent of the 192 participating national governments. This peaceful approach of not forcing anything on anyone is reproducing the status quo of increasing atmospheric concentrations of greenhouse gases. With every passing year, climate change is becoming more severe and urgent and more difficult to address. If we do not reverse course quickly, the positive feedbacks in the climate system—where more warming produces even more warming—will make catastrophic impacts inevitable.

We need to find a way to address climate change that goes beyond this war and peace. We need to exercise all of the political, law- and rule-making power of governments; all of the economic, product- and service-making power of business; and all of the cultural, meaning- and values-making power of civil society. And we need to exercise all of this power in the context of a loving unification across sectors, countries, and generations.

I can see the character of the challenge of climate change and of the response that is required of us. I cannot yet see how to mobilize that response in a way that is big enough and fast enough. But I have seen a fractal of what that response looks like.

In 2007, I met John Roy, a sixty-year-old real estate entrepreneur from Nova Scotia who was alarmed about climate change and especially about the woefully inadequate response of the Canadian government, and wanted to do something about it.

He wanted to make a high-leverage impact, even though he didn't have any experience either in climate change work or in Canadian public life. What he did have was a willingness to commit his resources: his credibility, his money, and above all his intentionality.

In the year that followed our first meeting, Roy went on, with help from me and my colleagues and others, to launch a series of initiatives aimed at moving Canada from being an international laggard to being a leader on actions to address climate change. These initiatives included a 3E (Economy, Energy, Environment) Alliance that brought together leaders of companies, environmental NGOs, academic institutions, and political parties, and a voter education campaign around climate change that was backed up by a public statement signed by seventy influential Canadians (including all but one of the country's living former prime ministers). One outcome of these efforts was that the Liberal Party (the official opposition in the national parliament) announced its support for a carbon tax, which was a radical and risky political move that the 3E Alliance viewed as key to making progress on climate change. Roy also launched a green industrial and office real estate company.

Roy's way of leading change was uncomfortable for some of the people involved, including me. A few of us discussed how we found him pushy and insensitive. But over the years, I had heard this same criticism about almost every one of the social change project initiators, around the world, with whom I had worked. To lead means to step forward, to exceed one's authority, to try to change the status quo, to exercise power, and such action is by definition disruptive. There is no way to change the status quo without discomforting those who are comfortable with the status quo.

Although I understood this consequence of working with both power and love, I was not prepared to deal with it personally. One meeting of the 3E Alliance was to be held at the Banff Centre, in the Rocky Mountains of Alberta. It was an excellent container for our work: a "social island" away from the hustle and bustle of the city, with views of and access to spacious and inspiring nature, encouraging both self-reflection and connection with others. It was also a symbolically significant location because Alberta is the center of Canada's oil and gas industry and will need to be part of any effective national approach to addressing climate change.

In the lead-up to this meeting, I observed an email exchange between Roy and a colleague. They were reviewing which of the competing politicians was coming to the meeting, what Roy should say or not say differently to each one, and how they could, paying attention to each participant's partisan interests, nudge him or her towards advancing 3E's agenda. I thought this approach was incompatible with our open and nonpartisan stance, and I became upset and threatened to quit the project. I eventually grasped that to work with both power and love requires working close-in and creatively, as Roy was doing, to align the self-realization of the whole (in this case of 3E and its climate change agenda) and the self-realization of each part (the participating individuals and their organizations).

Geographer Bent Flyvbjerg has drawn a similar conclusion from his studies of how power and rationality interact. His thesis, based on an in-depth study of urban policy and planning in the Danish town of Aalborg, is that neat rationality—reasoning through what is the best, true, loving solution to a given social problem—is by itself an inadequate basis for democratic problem solving, and that we must also engage with messy power:

> Power defines, and creates, concrete physical, economic, ecological, and social realities. Rationality is context-dependent, the context of rationality is power, and power blurs the dividing line between rationality and rationalization. We cannot rely solely on democracy based on rationality to solve our problems. Forms of participation that are practical, committed, and ready

for conflict provide a superior paradigm of democratic virtue than forms of participation that are discursive, detached, and consensus-dependent, that is, rational.[16]

This insight about the importance of close-in carving became clearer to me as I worked with the politicians who came to the 3E meetings. They chose to participate because they wanted to contribute to addressing the holistic challenge of climate change, but the parliamentary context from which they came was bruisingly partisan (etymologically: loyal to a part). One of them once said, "You all need to understand that I have come from an adversarial and competitive world, and I am not able to shift immediately to being transparent and trusting." The strength of 3E turned out to be not that it was nonpartisan but that it was multipartisan. Each participant—politician, businessperson, environmentalist, academic—was invited to bring his or her self-realizing part fully into the alliance, and together we would work through how to unite those parts into a greater whole that could address the climate challenge more effectively than any of us could alone.

During an Open Space session in one of our 3E workshops, I looked around the meeting room and saw four small groups, each contentedly engrossed in planning the initiative that they were going to work on after the workshop. I was struck that none of them was worried about what the other groups were going to do. They would listen to the others and try to be helpful, but they didn't need the approval of the others, and they trusted (given the understandings that they had built up) that all of the initiatives would basically be aligned. Each group realized its own initiative, in its own sphere of influence, in unforced unity with the others. The key shift that had occurred was a shift in members' language from "someone should" to "I will."

One of the characteristics of tough social challenges—that they are generatively complex—was coming into play. By definition, we cannot address challenges that are essentially unfamiliar

after enlightenment

and unpredictable simply by implementing an already-proven or already-worked-through plan. My partner Marianne Mille Bøjer suggests that faced with such overwhelming complexity we have two choices: to give up or to surrender.[17] Giving up means abandoning our effort to co-create new social realities and so reverting to either aggressive war or submissive peace. Surrendering means acknowledging that we can neither calculate nor control the outcome, and plunging into carving our way forward. Deng Xiaoping, the leader of the Chinese Communist Party, was referring to such an emergent approach when he explained the challenge of navigating China's unprecedented transition towards a socialist market economy: "We are crossing the river by feeling for stones."[18]

Most people find the prospect of employing an emergent approach to addressing their challenges to be unusual and daunting. But organizational theorist Karl Weick argues that in practice this is how people *usually* make progress in complex contexts:

> During military maneuvers in Switzerland, the young lieutenant of a small Hungarian detachment in the Alps sent a reconnaissance unit into the icy wilderness. It began to snow immediately, snowed for two days, and the unit did not return. The lieutenant suffered, fearing that he had dispatched his own people to death. But the third day the unit came back. Where had they been? How have they made their way? Yes, they said, we considered ourselves lost and waited for the end. And then one of us found a map in his pocket. That calmed us down. We pitched camp, lasted out the snowstorm, and then with the map we discovered our bearings. And here we are. The lieutenant borrowed this remarkable map and had a good look at it. He discovered to his astonishment that it was not a map of the Alps, but a map of the Pyrenees.[19]

Weick's argument is that people find their way forward not because they necessarily have a good strategy or map, but because they "begin to act, they generate tangible outcomes in some context, and this helps them discover what is occurring, what needs to be explained, and what should be done next."[20]

This is how many of the members of the 3E Alliance made their way forward. They understood that both the urgency and the generative complexity of the climate challenge implied that they had to step forward, even if their strategy and plan were imperfect or incomplete or not agreed to by everyone. They needed to get moving, to remain alert, and to learn and adjust as they went along. The alliance's meetings helped these participants move forward only partly because of the plans and agreements that they made. The primary benefit of these meetings was the creation of understandings, relationships, and energies that enabled participants to take their own next step forward with greater and more confident intentionality.

My partner Bill O'Brien used to say that distinguishing between generative and degenerative leadership is easy: if your boss is generative, you leave his or her office feeling lifted up, and if your boss is degenerative, you leave feeling dragged down. Distinguishing between a generative and degenerative social change effort is similarly easy. The 3E Alliance was generative inasmuch as many members left its meetings feeling lifted up and empowered.

The members of the 3E Alliance went as far as they could together. After one year, they disbanded the alliance and continued their climate change work in other configurations. In order to address our complex social challenges, we need many more such collaborative change initiatives.

How to Walk

An African proverb says, "If you want to walk fast, walk alone. If you want to walk far, walk together." Our tough social challenges increasingly require us to walk fast and far and together. When we are on smooth and familiar ground, we may be able to do this easily, even without paying attention. But in order to move forward fluidly on the uneven and unsteady and unfamiliar ground on which we increasingly find ourselves, we need a way to build our capacity for employing both our power and our love collectively.

How can we support the deliberate practice of collective walking in such complex contexts? By carefully constructing a container within which a team can address the tough social challenges that they all want to resolve but that none of them can resolve alone. By "container," I mean a physical, social, mental, and intentional place—what in Japanese is called *ba*.[21] Such a container must be at the same time both spacious enough and delimited enough to enable a team to experiment, play, and practice both creatively and safely.

A container can take many forms, including but not limited to variations of the change lab that my colleagues and I have been developing over the past decades. A *change lab* is a specific way for a diverse alliance of actors from across a given social system to work together to effect change in that system. They can do this locally (as the team did in Houston), nationally (Visión Guatemala), and/or internationally (the Sustainable Food Lab); with the intention of effecting change through new ideas (the Dinokeng Scenarios in South Africa), relationships (the Jewish Israeli Journey), and/or practical experiments (the 3E Alliance); over months (Destino Colombia) and/or years (the Bhavishya Alliance in India).

Gomathy Balasubramanian, Mia Eisenstadt, and Zaid Hassan describe it this way:

> The change lab is a controlled environment within which a group of people experience, become conscious of, and then develop strategies for how to cope with the

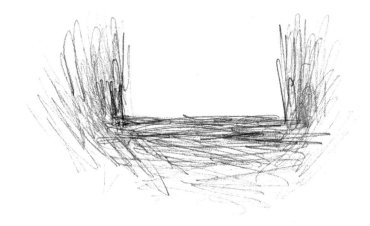

build a container

turbulent and fast-moving dynamics of a modern society. In comparison with the "real world," the change lab aspires to be a space within which it is safe to do things differently, be that shifting power relations or fostering a culture where mistakes are the basis of learning. The fast-changing nature of society today means that in some ways the strategies developed within the change lab are themselves less important than having the environment and the capacities with which to continually develop new strategies in response to the ebb and flow of social challenges.[22]

The essential activity of a change lab is a collective rhythmic repetition of the movements from power to love and back again. In the first movement, from power to love, we convene diverse actors who together are able to see and influence the system as a whole. We enable them to co-sense: to see and connect to more of the whole. In the Sustainable Food Lab, this first movement was accomplished through the processes of recruiting a team from across all parts of the food system, meeting as a group to share with one another, and going together on learning journeys to meet with and see from the perspectives of other actors in other parts of the system. One difficulty in effecting change in systems that are dynamically, socially, and generatively complex is that in these contexts we don't see causes and effects that are far away from us in time and space, perspectives that are radically different from our own, and an emerging reality that is essentially different from the one we are used to. The power-to-love processes help us overcome these three perceptual difficulties.

The movement from power to love enables actors to see more clearly the system that they are part of and their role in it. They see how they contribute to the system's producing the results it is producing and what—if they want the system to produce different results—they need to do differently. Boston College professor Bill Tolbert once remarked that the old quip "If you're not part of the solution, you're part of the problem" is less useful than the alternative formulation: "If you're not part of the problem, you can't be part of the solution."[23] Moving from power to love enables us to see more clearly how we are part of the problem and therefore how we can be part of the solution.

The second movement, from love to power, involves supporting actors to undertake individual and collective actions—arising out of and remaining in connection with their co-sensing of the whole of the system—to shift that system. It involves shifting from "someone should" to "I will." In the Food Lab, this second, co-realizing, movement was accomplished through processes that involved the members choosing to act: to join the lab and come to its meetings, to vote with their feet to join initiative teams, and to stay engaged in these initiatives through the long ups and downs of the practical work to create new social realities. The discomfort and conflict of the Salzburg meeting exemplified the challenge of stepping from love's connected feeling of warm belonging, to power's lonely feeling of putting on cold armor to do battle with the world, our colleagues, and ourselves.

In this two-movement framing of the change lab, the processes for co-presencing include both movements. In both the long retreat in Arizona and in the many shorter, spontaneous moments of collective insight (such as the five minutes in Guatemala), members of the Food Lab "let go" of their backward-looking separateness and attachment (thereby shifting from power to love) and "let come" their forward-looking, regenerated intention (shifting back from love to power). Co-presencing processes are important in reconciling the power-love dilemma because they enable us to enact our drive for self-realization in a context of a felt unity, and to enact our drive to unite in a context of pragmatic self-realization. The members of the Food Lab and of the 3E Alliance accomplished such reconciliations, but this did not mean that subsequently they were always successful—only that they had the requisite commitment to keep trying to move forward: to try and fail and learn and try again, over and over.

The change lab approach to co-creating new social realities involves building a container within which we can build up our capacity to walk fast and far together. This supports us in co-creating innovative ways to address our most complex challenges. It provides us with the time and space to breathe and stretch, to get confused and lost, to stumble and fall, and so to carve our way forward.

Conclusion:
To Lead Means to Step Forward

*W*HEN I LOOK BACK on the diverse social change teams I have worked with over the past twenty years, I notice one conclusion on which they all agreed: the complex and vital challenges we face cannot be addressed effectively by any one leader or organization or sector, and so we need to build our capacity for co-creation. The South African Dinokeng team gave this required approach to effecting social change a straightforward name: Walk Together.

In the previous chapters I have outlined the challenges, pitfalls, and requirements of walking together. But we cannot walk far and fast collectively if we cannot walk individually, on our own two feet. To contribute to co-creating new social realities, we have only one instrument: our selves. We cannot rely on others to effect change for us; nor can we, without violence, *get* others to change. If we want to exercise leadership in helping others progress from falling to stumbling to walking, we must be able to do so ourselves. If we want to exercise leadership in changing the world, we must be willing to change our selves.

I have understood this principle for a long time. My partner Bill O'Brien used to say, "The success of an intervention depends on the interior condition of the intervener." In India, businessman Arun Maira reminded me that the essence of what we were doing was "inviting stakeholder leaders to reflect on how they might need to change what they themselves are thinking and doing." But the fact that I understood how this principle applied to others didn't mean that I grasped what it implied for me and for my capacity to lead.

After I fell down at the end of the Bhavishya Lab, I spent months nursing my resentments against those I thought had pushed me. I knew I had made mistakes and needed to change, but I thought I was being unfairly singled out and others needed to change too: that I shouldn't be expected to work on myself unless others were doing the same. Then one day I came across a pamphlet written by the philosopher Martin Buber that challenged my position:

> This perspective, in which a man sees himself only as an individual contrasted with other individuals, and not as a genuine person whose transformation helps towards the transformation of the world, contains a fundamental error. The essential thing is to begin with oneself, and at this moment a man has nothing in the world to care about than this beginning. Any other attitude would distract him from what he is about to begin, weaken his initiative, and thus frustrate the entire bold undertaking.[1]

What does this "bold undertaking" of beginning with oneself mean in practice? It means working through in our individual actions the same progression from falling to stumbling to walking that I have described at the level of collective actions. First, we must pay attention to and keep in connection our power and our love. Second, we must balance ourselves by building up and bringing in our weaker drive. And third, we must practice moving forward through shifting fluidly between these two drives, so that they become one.

Becoming aware of both our power and our love

Our first step in learning to walk on our own two feet is to become aware of our own two-sided power and two-sided love. We can think of them in different ways—as masculine and feminine, agency and communion, left and right brain. We all have both these drives, but many of us have simplistically and mistakenly defaulted to paying attention to and relying on only one.[2] Psychologist Carl Jung advises, "Only what is separated may be properly joined."[3] So we must consciously and carefully observe both our power and our love, and neither confuse nor choose between nor forcibly fuse them. We must learn to live with the permanent reality, outside and within ourselves, of the creative tension presented by this dilemma. I have recounted the slow and unsteady broadening of my awareness of my power and love to help others recognize these two drives in themselves.

Balancing ourselves

Our second step in learning to walk is balancing ourselves by building up and bringing in our weaker drive. I have often found myself favoring one drive over the other and in this way to be unbalanced and hobbled—or more accurately, to have unbalanced and hobbled myself. On the one hand, when I am in conflict with someone and feel threatened and afraid of being hurt, I raise my defenses and withdraw. My ability to deal with the conflict further diminishes, my sense of the space I have to move contracts, and I become stuck: this is power attenuating uniting love. On the other hand, when I am enamored of uniting with another person or persons, I dare not move for fear that I will hurt them and disturb the unity: this is love attenuating self-realizing power.

When we are unbalanced, we stumble. When we are stumbling, we are not quite under control, and this feels unsteady and dangerous. But at least we are not falling: we are moving forward. Psychologist Robert Kegan suggests that the primary force driving all individual development is this "lifelong tension between the yearning to be independent and autonomous, to experience one's distinctiveness, the self-chosenness of one's directions, one's individual integrity, and the yearning to be included, to be part of, close to, joined with, to be held, admitted, accompanied."[4]

To keep moving forward, we need to be able to keep ourselves upright, to self-correct. We need to be able to prevent ourselves from going so far with our power that we lose touch with our love, or so far with our love that we lose touch with our power. This requires building up our awareness of and openness to feedback about how we are exercising our power and our love and with what results.

I once spoke with my colleague Tom Rautenberg when he was recovering from an illness that had resulted in his losing half of one of his feet. He had been in the hospital for four months, had had eight reconstructive operations, and was slowly learning to walk again. I asked him what he found most challenging in this process. He answered, "I have to unlearn consciously the habits that I learned to protect myself from hurting my damaged foot. I have to 're-member' my trust in the integrity of my own body, and my confidence and competence to move in the world. I have to regain my will to heal and to engage. This takes time and hard work." Healing our weaker drive requires us to unlearn consciously the habits that we have learned to protect ourselves from being hurt or from hurting others. This takes time and hard work.

In healing ourselves (and others), our wound becomes our gift. It points us to the part of ourselves that is sensitive and vulnerable and so requires our compassionate attention. Our willingness to recognize and admit our woundedness enables us to take the risk of stepping forward and stumbling or falling, and so to learn and grow. Rachel Naomi Remen, a medical doctor

your wound is your gift

who works with cancer patients, once said to me, "A shaman is someone who has a wound that will not heal. He sits by the side of the road with his open wound exposed. The stance of such a wounded healer is fundamentally different from that of an expert curer: the doctor in the clean white coat who stands, objective and healthy, above his patient." Our capacity to address our toughest social challenges depends on our willingness to admit that we are part of, rather than apart from, the woundedness of our world.

What holds us back from exercising all of our power and all of our love? Fear. Because we are afraid of offending or hurting others, we hold back our purposefulness and our power. Because we are afraid of being embarrassed or hurt, we hold back our openness and our love. We dysfunctionally allow our fears to prevent us from becoming whole.

Our way forward is not without these fears but through them. Leadership author Margaret Wheatley writes, "Fear is fundamental to being human, and so we can expect that we'll feel afraid at times, perhaps even frequently. What's important is to notice what we do with our fear. We can withdraw or distract or numb ourselves. Or we can recognize the fear, and then step forward anyway. Fearlessness simply means that we do not give fear the power to silence or stop us."[5] I once participated in a leadership training with family therapist Brenda Kerr in which, whenever students felt hurt or afraid and started to cry, Brenda would encourage them not to stop but rather to keep talking through their tears. We must not let our pain or fear prevent us from moving forward. Stepping forward means summoning the courage to step through our fear.

Although we may believe that fear helps us avoid getting hurt, often the opposite is true: we suffer more from trying to avoid pain than from pain itself. My own experience is that when I screw up my courage to undertake a social action that I fear will be terrible—to have a tough conversation, to make a connection, to step forward decisively—the result is usually better

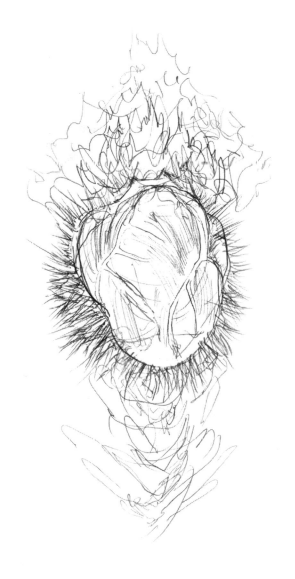

Courage

than I imagined or projected it would be. Author Jim Gimian once wrote, referring to his Tibetan Buddhist teacher Chögyam Trungpa, "Trungpa's teachings have lasting appeal because they speak to that place in people that 'sees what's really going on,' rather than to the place in people that hopes the bad news will all go away and clings unreasonably to the belief that we can all survive life's difficulties unscathed."[6] None of us can survive life's difficulties unscathed, but this does not mean that we ought fearfully to cover up and hide away our whole selves. Stepping forward means stepping up to becoming whole.

PRACTICING MOVING FLUIDLY

Our third step in learning to walk is to practice moving between power and love: to develop from unconscious incompetence to conscious incompetence to conscious competence to fluid unconscious competence. Such fluidity is neither rarefied nor rare: many people know how to move between power and love. I have observed fluid movement between power and love in many of the activists, entrepreneurs, politicians, facilitators, and artists with whom I have worked, and also, when I am at my best, in myself.

But many fewer people know how to move fluidly than know how to move only with power or only with love, and they are many fewer than are needed for us to adequately address our tough social challenges. More of us need to learn. To move fluidly is to be unstuck. My colleagues and I call our organization Reos Partners because *rheos* is the Greek word for "flow" or "stream."

I first noticed this capacity for fluid movement between power and love in an ordinary setting. I was in a restaurant with seasoned activist Michel Gelobter, and we were talking about our work on climate change. I kept focusing on the love dimension: how can we effectively address this problematic situation as a whole? Gelobter understood and embraced this dimension, but he also kept bringing the other dimension into the conversation—showing me by moving wineglasses and cutlery and salt and pepper shakers around on the tablecloth how each actor's interests and needs and power need to be understood, recognized, and taken into account. In observing his way of approaching this situation, I saw what practiced fluency in both power and love looks like.

I once taught a social change course at the Shambhala Institute for Authentic Leadership with my partner LeAnne Grillo and an Aikido master named Bob Wing. During one exercise, Wing asked the class to stand in a circle and invited a student to volunteer. He then set up the simplest possible social challenge: how could he get this student to move from one side of the circle to the other? First he pushed her, but this was not easy, and it left her resentful and waiting to retaliate. Then he promenaded her tantalizingly and gently from one side to another. After the exercise was over, he asked her offhandedly to move across the room, which she did willingly, not realizing that in doing so she had allowed him easily to achieve his objective of having her move to the other side of the circle; Wing didn't even point out to the class his winning move. Wing demonstrated that there is more than one way of addressing a given challenge and that some ways are less violent and more sustainable than others. "In Aikido," he told me, "what we aim to do is to be powerful and loving at the same time. Power does not mean hitting another person, and love does not mean giving up and hoping that the other will take care of us. I cannot throw a 200-pound person to the ground, but I can lead him into wanting to fall."

During the 3E Alliance meeting at the Banff Centre, I saw another example of fluid movement between power and love—this time among jazz musicians. The center hosts an annual international jazz school, and we invited a young trio called Fieldtrip to talk to us and demonstrate their musical collaboration. This turned out to be both informative and inspiring for our diverse and disagreement-laden alliance. Each of the musicians had his own particular background and strengths and music that he had practiced and wanted to show off. But when it came to playing together, their imperative was "Do everything to support and serve the music." United they could each better realize their own musical selves, and united they could realize music that was better than any of them could realize alone.

I have explored such processes for co-creation with my partner Jeff Barnum, who trained as a visual artist and who created the drawings in this book. He once showed me a film composed of a series of photographs taken as Pablo Picasso was painting a work entitled *Death of a Matador*.[7] Picasso did not implement an already-envisioned painting, but instead "found" the painting by putting paint down on the canvas and then painting over it, again and again and again. Jeff was pointing out that the process of creating something new in the world—be it a painting or a new social reality—requires us, not to plan it all out from the beginning, but rather to step forward, to act, to reflect on the results of our action, and then to take our next step. If we represent the journey from an existing reality to a new one along a U-shaped innovation path, we cannot stand at the beginning of the process and see the end: it is "around the corner." We have to step forward and meet the new reality along the way.

One aspect of the creative stance, Jeff suggests, is to have "a lot of intent without a lot of content." This stance is essential in co-creating new social realities because in this work we must be present and active but can neither predict nor control the outcome of our actions. Our context is too complex and emergent for any permanent solution to be possible. All we can do, and must do, is to unclench, pay attention, and take our best next step.

Discerning this next step requires both imagination and nonattachment to outcome. Such nonattachment does not guarantee that we will achieve our intention—but neither does hopeful attachment. (At an anxious moment in one of our workshops, Zaid Hassan helpfully counseled me, "Abandon hope.") The value of nonattachment is that it helps us to be less fearful and anxious, and so more open and creative. If we want to learn and move forward, we have to be willing to fail and fall.

Jim Gimian is the coauthor of two books about Sun Tzu's *The Art of War*.[8] In 2005, he was the first person to draw my attention to the blind spot in my thinking about power that was exposed in *Solving Tough Problems*. He asked me, "Why in your book are you so dismissive of force? Don't you realize that nothing in the world changes without the application of force? Force is in essence nothing more than the application of energy, without which change cannot happen. To be afraid of using force to be afraid of hurting anyone—is to be paralyzed into inaction. The important question is not whether to exercise force to effect change, but rather how to exercise force without aggression." He continued, giving an example from *The Art of War*:

> One of the key passages in this book is "One hundred victories in one hundred battles is not the most skillful. Subduing the other's military without battle is the most skillful." We translate this core challenge as "taking whole": how to achieve our objectives—be that vis-à-vis an opponent, a social imperative, or our own internal challenge—without destroying that for which we are fighting. Taking whole means acting on the basis of seeing things from the perspective of the whole.

Taking whole is a way beyond aggressive war and submissive peace. It involves employing our power and purposefulness to achieve the objective of our campaign while, inseparably, embracing with love our interconnected and interdependent situation. Journalist Larissa MacFarquar suggests that one source of Barack Obama's calm effectiveness is just this embrace: "If you take unity seriously, as Obama does, then outrage does not make sense, any more than it would make sense for a doctor to express outrage that a patient's kidney is causing pain in his back."[9]

Our power makes our love empowering instead of sentimental and anemic. Our love makes our power unifying instead of reckless and abusive. Our power and our love both become fuller and more generative, and the two intersuffuse and become one.

When I am facilitating at my best, I am using my power and my love to help the group use their power and their love: to grow and unite their self-realizing in the service of the self-realizing of the whole system of which they are a part. On one level, I am active and attentive—moving around at the front of the room, managing the agenda, inviting people to contribute, writing on flip charts, helping to synthesize and advance the content of the work. But at another level I am inactive and inattentive, present only to the emerging self-realization of the whole of the group and to my next step. I have intent without content. A participant in one of my workshops observed, "Beneath his visible activity, Adam has a deeper, quieter, intentional, invisible energy that is not really there and so is not a target. This is the energy that pulls us along."

The duality and unity of power and love constitute a mystery that we can approach and appreciate but cannot solve. When I first came across psychologist Robert Johnson's reference to the challenge of reconciling power and love, I searched in vain through his books for instructions on how to effect this reconciliation. The only hint he gives is a reference to the medieval Christian image of the mandorla:

> A mandorla is that almond-shaped segment that is made when two circles partly overlap. This symbol signifies nothing less than the overlap of the opposites that we have been investigating. The mandorla instructs us how to engage in reconciliation. It begins the healing of the split. The overlap generally is very tiny at first, only a sliver of the new moon; but it is a beginning. As time passes, the greater the overlap, the

greater and more complete is the healing. The mandorla binds together that which was torn apart and
made unwhole—unholy.[10]

We learn to walk by gradually becoming more conscious of
and present to both our power and our love, and allowing them
to overlap and the split between them to heal. Our power and
our love, which belong essentially together, energize and realize each other.

I have come to understand that the essence of the bold undertaking of beginning with myself is not so much to become someone different as it is to unfold my already-present potential. As I
have become more aware and balanced and fluid, I have become
more effective in leading. I still walk and stumble and fall, but
now with a greater capacity to notice and adjust and keep making my way forward.

STEPPING FORWARD

In June 2009, just as I was finishing up this book, I traveled again
to Colombia. My colleagues and I facilitated an energetic three-
day workshop of 150 top political, business, and civil society
leaders who had come together to work anew on a way forward
for their beautiful and wounded country. I was surprised and
delighted to see there many of my old friends from our 1997 Destino Colombia project and, even more so, to see that this prior
work, which I had understood had died without achieving its
desired impact, had in fact only been dormant. Over the inter-
vening twelve years, my friends and others had worked tirelessly
to keep moving toward the scenario of In Unity Lies Strength.
Now this work was flowering and inspiring a much larger group
of leaders to walk together.

At the end of the workshop, one of the organizers, peace activist Ana Teresa Bernal, exclaimed to me, "I can see now that what

we can do and are doing is co-creating a new reality for Colombia. It's like that poem of Antonio Machado: 'Walker, there is no path. The path is made by walking.'"[11]

So I have also come to understand that—contrary to my training in answering, controlling, and solving—social change work never produces final, ticked-off failure or success. Some social change efforts I thought were making progress later stalled, and some stalled efforts later made great advances. When Zhou Enlai, the first premier of the People's Republic of China, was asked in the early 1970s his assessment of the 1789 French Revolution, he replied, "It's too early to tell."[12] All we can do is try to keep moving forward, together, with increasing breadth and depth and sure-footedness.

In order to keep moving—and especially to lead such movement—we can and must make, and keep on making, only one simple choice: what is our next step?

My middle name is Moses, and so I have always been interested in the journey story of my biblical namesake. The Book of Exodus tells the story of Moses leading the Israelites out of Egypt and of the Red Sea parting so that they could cross towards the Promised Land. The Talmudic interpretation of this text contains the puzzling sentence that the first persons who stepped into the sea got their feet wet. During the workshop of the Jewish Israeli team in Eilat, beside the Red Sea, Rabbi Shlomo Pappenheim interpreted this for me by saying that when the Israelites got to the sea, it was not yet parted, and they sat on the bank and wailed for God to make a path for them. But then a young leader named Nahshon walked into the water, right up to his neck. It was this courageous act of stepping into the sea that created the path.

How can we learn to walk with power and love? The way is long, the terrain is rough, there is no path, and there is no map. We need companions on this journey, but no one else can make a way for us. We must use both of our legs; we must put one foot in front of the other. We must step forward.

into the sea

Notes

INTRODUCTION: BEYOND WAR AND PEACE

1. Jonathan Larson, *Rent: The Complete Book and Lyrics of the Broadway Musical* (New York: Applause Theatre and Cinema Books, 2008), 101. Tova Averbuch brought this intriguing formulation to my attention.

2. Paul Tillich, *Love, Power and Justice: Ontological Analyses and Ethical Applications* (New York: Oxford University Press, 1954), 25, 36.

3. Peter Senge and Claus Otto Scharmer, "Community Action Research" in *Handbook of Action Research*, ed. Peter Reason and Hilary Bradbury (Thousand Oaks, California: Sage Publications, 2001), 23.

4. I am indebted to Betty Sue Flowers for sharpening my understanding of the degenerative side of love.

5. Rollo May, *Love and Will* (New York: W. W. Norton & Co., 2007), 9, 14.

6. Martin Luther King Jr., "A Comparison of the Conceptions of God in the Thinking of Paul Tillich and Henry Nelson Wieman," in *The Papers of Martin Luther King, Jr., Volume II* (Berkeley: University of California Press, 1994), 339–544.

7. Martin Luther King Jr., "Where Do We Go From Here?" in *A Call to Conscience: The Landmark Speeches of Dr. Martin Luther King, Jr.*, ed. Clayborne Carson and Kris Shepherd (New York: Grand Central Publishing, 2002), 186.

8. Ibid., 187.

9. Carl Jung, *Two Essays in Analytical Psychology*, 2nd ed., trans. R. F. C. Hull (Princeton, New Jersey: Princeton University Press, 1966), 53.

10. Robert Johnson, *Owning Your Own Shadow: Understanding the Dark Side of the Psyche* (New York: HarperOne, 1993), 89.

CHAPTER 1: THE TWO SIDES OF POWER

1. This point about the dominance in many spheres of the competitive meme was made to me by Mary Catherine Bateson.

2. King, "Where Do We Go From Here?" 185.

3. Arie de Geus, *The Living Company: Habits for Survival in a Turbulent Business Environment* (Cambridge, Massachusetts: Harvard Business School Press, 2002).

4. See Kahane, *Solving Tough Problems: An Open Way of Talking, Listening, and Creating New Realities* (San Francisco: Berrett-Koehler, 2004), 19–33, 79–83; Pieter le Roux et al., "The Mont Fleur Scenarios," *Deeper News* 7, no. 1 (Emeryville, California: Global Business Network, 1992); Glennifer Gillespie, "The Mont Fleur Scenario Project, South Africa, 1991-1992: The Footprints of Mont Fleur" in *Civic Scenario/Civic Dialogue Workshop*, ed. Bettye Pruitt (New York: United Nations Development Programme Regional Bureau for Latin America and the Caribbean, 2000); and Nick Segal, *Breaking the Mould: The Role of Scenarios in Shaping South Africa's Future* (Stellenbosch, South Africa: Sun Press, 2007) .

5. Kahane, *Solving Tough Problems*, 82.

6. Tillich, *Love, Power and Justice*, 47.

7. Steven Lukes, *Power: A Radical View*, 2nd ed. (New York: Palgrave Macmillan, 2005), 12.

8. California attorney general Bill Lockyer, quoted in *The California Electricity Crisis*, James Sweeney (Stanford, California: Hoover Institution Press, 2002), 192.

9. Quoted in the trailer to *The Queen, The Rabbi & The Lama: Exploring The Heart of Compassionate Leadership*, directed by James Hoagland, 2008.

10. Personal communication with Ursula Versteegen.

11. Richard Pratt, *Official Report of the Nineteenth Annual Conference of Charities and Correction* (1892), reprinted in *Americanizing the American Indians: Writings by the "Friends of the Indian" 1880-1900*, ed. Francis Prucha (Cambridge, Massachusetts: Harvard University Press, 1973), 260–271.

12. See Kevin Keefe, *Paddy's Road: Life Stories of Patrick Dodson* (Canberra: Aboriginal Studies Press, 2003).

13. *The White Planet*, directed by Thierry Ragobert and Thierry Piantanida, 2007.

14. *Kanyini*, directed by Melanie Hogan, 2006.

15. Elizabeth Kolbert, "Greening the Ghetto," *New Yorker*, January 12, 2009, 25.

CHAPTER 2: THE TWO SIDES OF LOVE

1. Peter Senge, *The Fifth Discipline: The Art & Practice of the Learning Organization* (New York: Broadway Business, 2006).

2. William J. O'Brien, *Character at Work: Building Prosperity Through the Practice of Virtue* (Boston: Paulist Press, 2008), viii.

3. Ibid., 105.

4. Humberto Maturana and Pille Bunnell, "The Biology of Business: Love Expands Intelligence," *Reflections* (1999): 2.

5. Robert Johnson, *We: Understanding the Psychology of Romantic Love* (New York: HarperOne, 1983), 191.

6. See Kahane, *Solving Tough Problems*, 113–127, and Elena Díez, "Visión Guatemala, 1998-2000: Building Bridges of Trust," in *Civic Scenario/ Civic Dialogue Workshop*, ed. Pruitt.

7. Díez, "Visión Guatemala," 30.

8. Maturana and Bunnell, "The Biology of Business," 1.

9. Thais Corral helped me see the connection between my weaving and my mother's.

10. I am indebted to Hugo Beteta for this insight about what it means to have a gift.

11. Peter Senge, Otto Scharmer, Joseph Jaworski, and Betty Sue Flowers, *Presence: Human Purpose and the Field of the Future* (New York: Broadway Business, 2008), 189.

12. Joseph Jaworski, *Synchronicity: The Inner Path of Leadership* (San Francisco: Berrett-Koehler, 1996).

13. Otto Scharmer, *Theory U: Leading from the Future as It Emerges* (San Francisco: Berrett-Koehler, 2009).

14. See Kahane, *Solving Tough Problems*, 59–65; Manuel José Carvajal, et al., "Destino Colombia: A Scenario-Planning Process for the New Millennium," *Deeper News* 9, no. 1 (Emeryville, California: Global Business Network, 1998); Alfredo de León and Elena Díez, "Destino Colombia, 1997–2000: A Treasure to Be Revealed," in *Civic Scenario/ Civic Dialogue Workshop*; and Angelika Rettberg, *Destino Colombia: Crónica y evaluación de un ejercicio de participación de líderes de la sociedad civil en el diseño de escenarios futuros* (Bogotá: Ediciones Uniandes, 2006).

15. Personal communication with Antanas Mockus.

16. Paulo Freire, *The Politics of Education: Culture, Power and Liberation* (Westport, Connecticut: Bergin & Garvey, 1985), 122.

17. Personal communication with Clara Arenas.

18. Tillich, *Love, Power and Justice*, 50–51.

19. Scharmer, *Theory U*, 39.

20. James Hillman, *Kinds of Power: A Guide to Its Intelligent Uses* (New York: Doubleday, 1995), 108.

21. Quoted in Marvin Weisbord, *Discovering Common Ground: How Future Search Conferences Bring People Together to Achieve Breakthrough Innovation, Empowerment, Shared Vision, and Collaborative Action* (San Francisco: Berrett-Koehler, 1992), 23.

CHAPTER 3: THE DILEMMA OF POWER AND LOVE

1. Charles Hampden-Turner, *Charting the Corporate Mind* (New York: Blackwell Publishing, 1993).

2. Ibid., 107.

3. Ibid., 125.

4. Tillich, *Love, Power and Justice*, 12.

CHAPTER 4: FALLING

1. United Nations Children's Fund, *State of the World's Children* (New York: UNICEF, 2008).

2. I learned this from Louis van der Merwe.

3. Johan Galtung, Peace by *Peaceful Means: Peace and Conflict, Development and Civilization* (London: Sage Publications, 1996), 31.

4. See Arun Maira, *Shaping the Future: Leadership through Communities of Aspiration in India and Beyond* (New York: Wiley, 2002).

5. Gomathy Balasubramanian, Mia Eisenstadt, and Zaid Hassan, "The Birth of the Bhavishya Alliance: Learnings & Insights" (unpublished paper, 2007, 11).

6. Ibid., 28.

7. Ibid., 16–17.

8. *The Road to Bhavishya*, directed by Paromita Bora, 2007.

9. Balasubramanian, Eisenstadt, and Hassan, "The Birth of the Bhavishya Alliance," 29.

10. *The Road to Bhavishya*.

11. Edwin Friedman, *A Failure of Nerve: Leadership in the Age of the Quick Fix* (New York: Seabury Books, 2007), 254.

12. See Myrna Lewis, *Inside the NO: Five Steps to Decisions that Last* (London: Indranet, 2009).

13. Weisbord, *Discovering Common Ground*, 7.

14. See www.bhavishya.org.in.

CHAPTER 5: STUMBLING

1. This team consisted of Tova Averbuch, Hilik Bar, Avner Haramati, Baruch Ovadia, Mario Schejtman, Shay Ben Yosef, and Ofer Zalzberg.

2. Harrison Owen, *A Brief User's Guide to Open Space Technology* (San Francisco: Berrett-Koehler, 2008), 95.

3. Abraham Joshua Heschel, *The Sabbath* (New York: Farrar Straus Giroux, 2005).

4. Tillich, *Love, Power and Justice*, 25.

5. Personal communication with Tova Averbuch.

6. See Barry Oshry, *Seeing Systems: Unlocking the Mysteries of Organizational Life* (San Francisco: Berrett-Koehler, 2007).

7. Barry Oshry, "Power Without Love and Love Without Power: A Systems Perspective" (unpublished paper, 2009).

8. John Gardner, *On Leadership* (New York: Free Press, 1993), 95.

9. Personal communication with Tova Averbuch.

10. See www.dinokengscenarios.co.za.

11. Johnson, *We*, 193.

12. See Kees van der Heijden, *Scenarios: The Art of Strategic Conversation* (West Sussex: John Wiley, 1996).

13. Zaid Hassan, "Bhavishya Reflections" (unpublished paper, October 2006); see also Zaid Hassan, *Laboratories for Social Change*, forthcoming in 2010.

14. See William Isaacs, *Dialogue: The Art of Thinking Together* (New York: Broadway Business, 1999), 226.

15. Crane Stookey, "The Container Principle: Resilience, Chaos and Trust" (Halifax: The Nova Scotia Sea School, 2003), 3.

16. Personal communication with Gabrielle Rifkind.

17. Edward Chambers and Michael Cowan, *Roots for Radicals: Organizing for Power, Action, and Justice* (New York: Continuum, 2003), 28.

18. Ibid., 30–31.

19. John Carlin, *Playing the Enemy: Nelson Mandela and the Game that Made a Nation* (London: Atlantic Books, 2008), 221–222.

20. Ibid., 120.

21. I am indebted to Louis van der Merwe for this definition of health.

Chapter 6: Walking

1. Vandana Shiva, "Tierra Madre: A Celebration of Living Economies," in *Manifestos on the Future of Food & Seed* (Cambridge, Massachusetts: South End Press, 2007), 1.

2. See www.sustainablefoodlab.org.

3. Hal Hamilton, "The Story of the Sustainable Food Lab" (unpublished paper, March 2009, 3).

4. Susan Sweitzer, "Sustainable Food Lab Learning History Chapter 2" (unpublished paper, 2004, 12).

5. Ibid., 24.

6. Brian Arthur, *The Nature of Technology: What It Is and How It Evolves* (New York: Free Press, 2009).

7. Personal communication with Angela Wilkinson.

8. Personal communication with Mari Fitzduff.

9. Sweitzer, "Sustainable Food Lab," 35.

10. Kahane, *Solving Tough Problems*, 80.

11. Hamilton, "The Story of the Sustainable Food Lab," 11.

12. Ibid., 1.

13. Peter Senge, "The Life Cycle of Typical Change Initiatives," in *The Dance of Change: The Challenges to Sustaining Momentum in Learning Organizations*, by Peter Senge, Art Kleiner, Charlotte Roberts, George Roth, Rick Ross, and Bryan Smith (New York: Broadway Business, 1999), 8.

14. See Buckminster Fuller Institute, www.bfi.org.

15. Personal communication with Earl Saxon.

16. Bent Flyvbjerg, *Rationality and Power: Democracy in Practice* (Chicago: University of Chicago Press, 1998), 227–236.

17. Personal communication with Marianne Mille Bøjer.

18. Quoted in Barbara Heinzen, *Feeling for Stones: Learning and Invention When Facing the Unknown* (London: Author, 2006).

19. Karl Weick, *Making Sense of the Organization* (Oxford: Blackwell Publishing, 2001), 345–346.

20. Ibid., 346.

21. Scharmer, *Theory U*, 463.

22. Balasubramanian, Eisenstadt, and Hassan, "The Birth of the Bhavishya Alliance," 6.

23. Personal communication with Bill Tolbert.

Conclusion: To Lead Means to Step Forward

1. Martin Buber, *The Way of Man According to the Teachings of Hasidism* (Wallingford, Pennsylvania: Pendle Hill Publications, 1960), 21.

2. Jill Bolte Taylor, a neuroanatomist, suggests a neurological basis for the dual capacities for power and love. Ten years ago, Taylor had a stroke and completely lost the functioning of the left hemisphere of her brain. For three weeks she had the unusual experience of functioning with only her right hemisphere. In her report of this experience, she says, "The two hemispheres process information differently;

each hemisphere thinks about different things, they care about different things, and dare I say, they have very different personalities. The left hemisphere is that little voice that says to me, 'I am. I am.' And as soon as my left hemisphere says to me 'I am,' I become separate." So in the language of this book, the left hemisphere is the brain of self-realization, of power. Taylor goes on to report, "The right hemisphere says, 'We are energy beings connected to one another as one human family. We are perfect. We are whole. And we are beautiful.'" So in the language of this book, the right hemisphere is the brain of unity, of love. See Jill Bolte Taylor, "My Stroke of Insight," speech to the TED Conference, Monterey, California, February 27, 2008.

3. Johnson, *We*, 49.

4. Robert Kegan, *The Evolving Self: Problem and Process in Human Development* (Cambridge, Massachusetts: Harvard University Press, 1982), 107.

5. See Margaret Wheatley, *Turning to One Another: Simple Conversations to Restore Hope to the Future* (San Francisco: Berrett-Koehler, 2009), 152.

6. Personal communication with Jim Gimian.

7. *The Mystery of Picasso*, directed by Henri-Georges Clouzot, 1956.

8. James Gimian and Barry Boyce, *The Rules of Victory: How to Transform Chaos and Conflict—Strategies from "The Art of War"* (Boston: Shambhala Press, 2008), and Sun Tzu, *The Art of War: The Denma Translation*, trans. Kidder Smith and James Gimian (Boston: Shambhala Press, 2002).

9. Larissa MacFarquar, "The Conciliator," *New Yorker*, May 7, 2007, 49.

10. Johnson, *Owning Your Own Shadow*, 89–102.

11. "Caminante, no hay camino, se hace camino al andar." Antonio Machado, *Antologia Poetica Machado* (Alfaguara, Madrid: 2005), 92.

12. Chun Lin, *The Transformation of Chinese Socialism* (Durham, North Carolina: Duke University Press, 2006), 164.

Bibliography

Arthur, Brian. *The Nature of Technology: What It Is and How It Evolves.* New York: Free Press, 2009.

Balasubramanian, Gomathy, Mia Eisenstadt, and Zaid Hassan. "The Birth of the Bhavishya Alliance: Learnings & Insights" (unpublished paper, 2007).

Buber, Martin. *The Way of Man According to the Teachings of Hasidism.* Wallingford, Pennsylvania: Pendle Hill Publications, 1960.

Carlin, John. *Playing the Enemy: Nelson Mandela and the Game that Made a Nation.* London: Atlantic Books, 2008.

Carson, Clayborne, and Kris Shepherd. *A Call to Conscience: The Landmark Speeches of Dr. Martin Luther King, Jr.* New York: Grand Central Publishing, 2002.

Carvajal, Manuel José, et al. "Destino Colombia: A Scenario-Planning Process for the New Millennium." *Deeper News* 9, no. 1 (1998).

Chambers, Edward, and Michael Cowan. *Roots for Radicals: Organizing for Power, Action, and Justice.* New York: Continuum, 2003.

De Geus, Arie. *The Living Company: Habits for Survival in a Turbulent Business Environment.* Cambridge, Massachusetts: Harvard Business School Press, 2002.

Flyvbjerg, Bent. *Rationality and Power: Democracy in Practice.* Chicago: University of Chicago Press, 1998.

Freire, Paulo. *The Politics of Education: Culture, Power and Liberation.* Westport, Connecticut: Bergin & Garvey, 1985.

Friedman, Edwin. *A Failure of Nerve: Leadership in the Age of the Quick Fix.* New York: Seabury Books, 2007.

Galtung, Johan. *Peace by Peaceful Means: Peace and Conflict, Development and Civilization.* London: Sage Publications, 1996.

Gardner, John. *On Leadership.* New York: Free Press, 1993.

Gimian, James, and Barry Boyce. *The Rules of Victory: How to Transform Chaos and Conflict—Strategies from "The Art of War".* Boston: Shambhala Press, 2008.

Hamilton, Hal. "The Story of the Sustainable Food Lab" (unpublished paper, March 2009).

Hampden-Turner, Charles. *Charting the Corporate Mind.* New York: Blackwell Publishing, 1993.

Hassan, Zaid. *Laboratories for Social Change* (forthcoming in 2010).

———. "Bhavishya Reflections" (unpublished paper, October 2006).

Heinzen, Barbara. *Feeling for Stones: Learning and Invention When Facing the Unknown.* London: Author, 2006.

Heschel, Abraham Joshua. *The Sabbath.* New York: Farrar Straus Giroux, 2005.

Hillman, James. *Kinds of Power: A Guide to Its Intelligent Uses.* New York: Doubleday, 1995.

Isaacs, William. *Dialogue: The Art of Thinking Together.* New York: Broadway Business, 1999.

Jaworski, Joseph. *Synchronicity: The Inner Path of Leadership.* San Francisco: Berrett-Koehler, 1996.

Johnson, Robert. *Owning Your Own Shadow: Understanding the Dark Side of the Psyche.* New York: HarperOne, 1993.

———. *We: Understanding the Psychology of Romantic Love.* New York: HarperOne, 1983.

Jung, Carl. *Two Essays in Analytical Psychology,* 2nd ed. Trans. R. F. C. Hull. Princeton, New Jersey: Princeton University Press, 1966.

Kahane, Adam. *Solving Tough Problems: An Open Way of Talking, Listening, and Creating New Realities.* San Francisco: Berrett-Koehler, 2004.

Keefe, Kevin. *Paddy's Road: Life Stories of Patrick Dodson.* Canberra: Aboriginal Studies Press, 2003.

Kegan, Robert. *The Evolving Self: Problem and Process in Human Development.* Cambridge, Massachusetts: Harvard University Press, 1982.

King, Martin Luther, Jr. *The Papers of Martin Luther King, Jr., Volume II.* Berkeley: University of California Press, 1994.

Kolbert, Elizabeth. "Greening the Ghetto." *New Yorker* (January 12, 2009).

Larson, Jonathan. *Rent: The Complete Book and Lyrics of the Broadway Musical.* New York: Applause Theatre and Cinema Books, 2008.

Le Roux, Pieter, et al. "The Mont Fleur Scenarios." *Deeper News* 7, no. 1 (1992).

Lewis, Myrna. *Inside the NO: Five Steps to Decisions that Last.* London: Indranet, 2009.

Lin, Chun. *The Transformation of Chinese Socialism.* Durham, North Carolina: Duke University Press, 2006.

Lukes, Steven. *Power: A Radical View*, 2nd ed. New York: Palgrave Macmillan, 2005.

MacFarquar, Larissa. "The Conciliator." *New Yorker* (May 7, 2007).

Machado, Antonio. *Antologia Poetica Machado.* Alfaguara, Madrid: 2005., page 92.

Maira, Arun. *Shaping the Future: Leadership through Communities of Aspiration in India and Beyond.* New York: Wiley, 2002.

Maturana, Humberto, and Pille Bunnell. "The Biology of Business: Love Expands Intelligence." *Reflections* (1999).

May, Rollo. *Love and Will.* New York: W. W. Norton & Co., 2007.

O'Brien, William J. *Character at Work: Building Prosperity Through the Practice of Virtue.* Boston: Paulist Press, 2008.

Oshry, Barry. *Seeing Systems: Unlocking the Mysteries of Organizational Life.* San Francisco: Berrett-Koehler, 2007.

———. "Power Without Love and Love Without Power: A Systems Perspective" (unpublished paper, 2009).

Owen, Harrison. *Open Space Technology: A User's Guide.* San Francisco: Berrett-Koehler, 2008.

Prucha, Francis, ed. *Americanizing the American Indians: Writings by the "Friends of the Indian" 1880–1900.* Cambridge, Massachusetts: Harvard University Press, 1973.

Pruitt, Bettye, ed. *Civic Scenario/Civic Dialogue Workshop.* New York: United Nations Development Programme Regional Bureau for Latin America and the Caribbean, 2000.

Reason, Peter, and Hilary Bradbury, eds. *Handbook of Action Research.* Thousand Oaks, California: Sage Publications, 2001.

Rettberg, Angelika. *Destino Colombia: Crónica y evaluación de un ejercicio de participación de líderes de la sociedad civil en el diseño de escenarios futuros.* Bogotá: Ediciones Uniandes, 2006.

Scharmer, Otto. *Theory U: Leading from the Future as It Emerges.* San Francisco: Berrett-Koehler, 2009.

Segal, Nick. *Breaking the Mould: The Role of Scenarios in Shaping South Africa's Future.* Stellenbosch, South Africa: Sun Press, 2007.

Senge, Peter. *The Fifth Discipline: The Art & Practice of the Learning Organization.* New York: Broadway Business, 2006.

Senge, Peter, Art Kleiner, Charlotte Roberts, George Roth, Rick Ross, and Bryan Smith. *The Dance of Change: The Challenges to Sustaining Momentum in Learning Organizations.* New York: Broadway Business, 1999.

Senge, Peter, Otto Scharmer, Joseph Jaworski, and Betty Sue Flowers. *Presence: Human Purpose and the Field of the Future.* New York: Broadway Business, 2008.

Shiva, Vandana. "Tierra Madre: A Celebration of Living Economies." In *Manifestos on the Future of Food & Seed.* Cambridge, Massachusetts: South End Press, 2007.

Stookey, Crane. "The Container Principle: Resilience, Chaos and Trust." Halifax: The Nova Scotia Sea School, 2003.

Sun, Tzu. *The Art of War: The Denma Translation.* Trans. Kidder Smith and James Gimian. Boston: Shambhala Press, 2002.

Sweeney, James. *The California Electricity Crisis.* Stanford, California: Hoover Institution Press, 2002.

Sweitzer, Susan. "Sustainable Food Lab Learning History Chapter 2" (unpublished paper, 2004).

Taylor, Jill Bolte. "My Stroke of Insight" (speech to the TED Conference, Monterey, California, February 27, 2008).

Tillich, Paul. *Love, Power and Justice: Ontological Analyses and Ethical Applications.* New York: Oxford University Press, 1954.

United Nations Children's Fund. *State of the World's Children.* New York: UNICEF, 2008.

Van der Heijden, Kees. *Scenarios: The Art of Strategic Conversation.* West Sussex: John Wiley, 1996.

Weick, Karl. *Making Sense of the Organization.* Oxford: Blackwell Publishing, 2001.

Weisbord, Marvin. *Discovering Common Ground: How Future Search Conferences Bring People Together to Achieve Breakthrough Innovation, Empowerment, Shared Vision, and Collaborative Action.* San Francisco: Berrett-Koehler, 1992.

Wheatley, Margaret. *Turning to One Another: Simple Conversations to Restore Hope to the Future.* San Francisco: Berrett-Koehler, 2009.

Acknowledgments

ADAM KAHANE

This book has grown out of twenty years of conversations—lighthearted and tense, extended and in passing, at work and at play—with colleagues, friends, and family. Without these conversations and the relationships from which they arose there would be no book, and to these people I owe an enormous debt of gratitude. Not all of them agree with all of my interpretations of the events we lived through together, nor with all of the conclusions I have drawn. For these interpretations and conclusions and for any deficiencies in this book (including omissions from these acknowledgments), I take full responsibility.

Much of my learning has been in the context of the social change projects described in this book. Every one of these initiatives is a testimony to the power of other-centered leadership, including that exercised by, in the Bhavishya Alliance, Priya Aherwar, Suryakant Badgeri, Gomathy Balasubramanian, Isha Bhagwat, Paromita Bora, Sudha Cannan, Peggy Dulany, Kiran Gulrajani, Prativa Gulrajani, Tex Gunning, Zaid Hassan, Joseph Jaworski, Arun Maira, Joe McCarron, Vinod Nair, Ujjwala Pendse, Tom Rautenberg, Surita Sandosham, C. V. Sharma, M. K. Sharma, Venkatram Srinivas, Manish Srivastava, Pallavi Varma-Patil, Paulus Verschuren, and David Winder; in Destino Colombia and Evolución Colombia, J. Mario Aristizabal,

Jeff Barnum, Ana Teresa Bernal, Hans Blumenthal, Manuel José Carvajal, Hugo Estrada, Manuel Manga, Joe McCarron, Antanas Mockus, Germán Montoya, Joaquín Moreno, Inés de Mosquera, Gustavo Mutis, and Luis Sandoval; on the Dinokeng Scenarios, Sarah Babb, Matt Bland, Pippa Green, Bob Head, Graça Machel, Itumeleng Mahabane, Alayne Mannion, Vincent Maphai, Debra Marsden, Rick Menell, Ishmael Mkhabela, Yvonne Muthien, Njongonkulu Ndungane, and Mamphela Ramphele; on the Jewish Israeli Journey, Tova Averbuch, Ahmed Badawi, Hilik Bar, Shay Ben Yosef, Avner Haramati, Baruch Ovadia, Gabrielle Rifkind, Mario Schejtman, and Ofer Zalzberg; on the Mont Fleur Scenario Exercise, Dorothy Kahane, Koosum Kalyan, Vincent Maphai, and Pieter le Roux; in the Sustainable Food Lab, Arie van den Brand, Nancy Gabriel, LeAnne Grillo, Hal Hamilton, Zaid Hassan, Oran Hesterman, Joseph Jaworski, Daniella Malin, Joe McCarron, Tacito Nobre, Tom Rautenberg, Alison Sander, Peter Senge, Don Seville, Susan Sweitzer, Susan Taylor, Jan-Kees Vis, Pierre Vuarin, and Alain Wouters; in the 3E Alliance, LeAnne Grillo, Joe McCarron, Ted Parson, and John Roy; and in Visión Guatemala, Clara Arenas, Bety de Bernal, Ana Carpio, Elena Díez, Anaì Linares, Reola Phelps, and Ricardo Stein.

I have worked on all of these projects (except Mont Fleur) as a member of Reos Partners and its predecessor organization Generon Consulting. I have been able to contribute to co-creating new social realities in these project spaces because of the co-creative spaces we have built in these partnerships. My partners have both challenged and embraced me, through thick and thin; I am deeply grateful for their integrity and generosity. They include, in Reos Partners, Sarah Babb, Jeff Barnum, Marianne Mille Bøjer, Mia Eisenstadt, LeAnne Grillo, Zaid Hassan, Marianne Knuth, Colleen Magner, Joe McCarron, Vanessa Sayers, and Mustafa Suleyman; and in Generon Consulting, LeAnne Grillo, Cari Godbois, Zaid Hassan, Nancy Hopkins, Joseph Jaworski, Joe McCarron, Grady

McGonagill, Reola Phelps, Tom Rautenberg, Wick Sloane, Janice Spadafore, Susan Taylor, Vicki Tweiten, Margaret Vaughan, and the late Bill O'Brien.

I have also had the privilege of being a member of and visitor to several outstanding groups of professionals and scholars who have, formally and informally, helped me develop the ideas in this book. They include, in the Brookline Group, Lee Bolman, David Brown, Tim Hall, Todd Jick, Bill Kahn, Phil Mirvis, and Barry Oshry; at the Community Development Resource Association, Allan Kaplan and James Taylor; at Global Business Network, Napier Collyns, Katherine Fulton, Gerald Harris, Barbara Heinzen, Nancy Murphy, Jay Ogilvy, and Peter Schwartz; in the Global Leadership Network, Dalberto Adulis, Thais Corrall, Mari Fitzduff, Ernie Garilao, Alain Gauthier, Mark Gerzon, Walter Link, Helio Mattar, Paola Melchiori, Rachel Naomi Remen, and Bill Ury; at the International Futures Forum, Napier Collyns, Kees van der Heijden, Graham Leicester, Andrew Lyon, Arun Maira, and Maureen O'Hara; at Naropa University, Susan Skjei and Mark Wilding; at Pegasus Communications, Janice Molloy and Ginny Wiley; at the Presencing Institute and the Society for Organizational Learning, Mary Catherine Bateson, Maria D'Arce, Glennifer Gillespie, Beth Jandernoa, Katrin Kaeufer, Nina Kruschwitz, Sherry Immediato, Bettye Pruitt, Otto Scharmer, Ed Schein, Peter Senge, Bill Torbert, and Ursula Versteegen; at the Synergos Institute, Peggy Dulany, Bob Dunn, John Heller, Surita Sandosham, Bruce Schearer, and Barry Smith; at the University of Oxford, Rafael Ramirez, Deborah Ravetz, and Angela Wilkinson; at the Shambhala Institute for Authentic Leadership, Phil Cass, Michael Chender, Elizabeth Clement, Jim Gimian, Danny Graham, Jerry Granelli, Arawana Hayashi, Susan Szpakowski, Meg Wheatley, and Bob Wing; and in other settings, Zafer Achi, Brian Arthur, Clare Beckton, David Chrislip, David Diamond, Patrick Dodson, Bo Ekman, David Fine, Betty Sue Flowers, Dominique Gabella, Michel

Gelobter, Erika Gregory, Larry Horwitz, David Kahane, Brenda Kerr, Paul Lane, Myrna Lewis, Louis van der Merwe, John Milton, Denny Minno, Jerry Nagel, Njabulo Ndebele, Barbara Nussbaum, Howard Pedersen, Nicanor Perlas, Morris Rosenberg, Karen Rowantree, Earl Saxon, Nick Segal, Judy Tal, Jorge Talavera, Philip Thomas, Gene Vaughan, Rosa Walker, Frances Westley, and Phyllis Woolley.

A particular kindness has been shown to me by the people who took the time to read and comment on drafts of this book (some of them several times), including Tova Averbuch, Jeff Barnum, Marianne Mille Bøjer, Manuel José Carvajal, Michael Chender, Elena Díez, Sandra Dunsmore, Mia Eisenstadt, Michel Gelobter, Jim Gimian, LeAnne Grillo, Avner Haramati, Zaid Hassan, Philip Heller, Bernard Kahane, David Kahane, Dorothy Kahane, Naomi Kahane, Jeffrey Kulick, Colleen Magner, Joe McCarron, Grady McGonagill, Gustavo Mutis, Bettye Pruitt, Tom Rautenberg, Gabrielle Rifkind, Adryan Russ, Earl Saxon, Jill Swenson, Susan Taylor, Philip Thomas, Jim Williams, and Ofer Zalzberg.

One of the most enjoyable parts of preparing this book has been, as before, working with the people of Berrett-Koehler, including Maria Jesus Aguilo, Henrietta Bensussen, Judith Brown, Peter Cavagnaro, Michael Crowley, Kristen Franz, Linda Jupiter, Medea Minnich, Dianne Platner, Jeevan Sivasubramaniam, Jeremy Sullivan, Richard Wilson, and especially Steve Piersanti.

Finally, I would like to thank my family, for all of their loving and empowering encouragement and forbearance: Allan Jr. and Pulane Boesak; Bernard, David, Jed, and Naomi Kahane; Caelin, Daniel, Joshua, and Lieneke Thyssen; Belen, Ciaran, J.P., and Siobhan Wilkinson; and above all Dorothy.

Jeff Barnum

I would like to acknowledge William Pope.L, an inimitable artist who profoundly, earnestly, and humorously pictures the racial divide in America. He showed me how to develop a drawing practice that is the basis of all my creative and professional work. Thanks to Dennis Klocek, my friend and mentor, who urged me countless times over many years to start drawing. Whoever sees anything of value in my drawings sees also Dennis's impact on my life and person. Thanks to my friend Andrew Sullivan, one of the first people to recognize and appreciate my efforts. Thanks also to my family: my parents Sue and Dan, my sister Betsy, my grandfather Glenn who always encouraged me to become me, and most of all to my life partner Louisa and our daughters Iren and Farranika. Louisa has repeatedly appreciated the quality of line in my drawings and thus indirectly amplified that line's livingness, energy, and precision. Finally, I would like to acknowledge my friends and colleagues in Reos Partners. I look forward to every day of our walking together.

Index

aboriginal peoples, 4, 22–23, 25–26, 32, 109

affirmative action, 24, 98

African National Congress, 16, 17, 87, 96, 99

Akatu, 113

akatu (seed; world), 113

Alberta, 116–117

Alinsky, Saul, 94

American Leadership Forum, 36

apartheid (apartness), 13, 18, 91, 96, 97

Arabs, 76, 77, 78, 80

Arenas, Clara, 45–46

Art of War (Sun Tzu), 137

Arthur, Brian, 37, 108

Arthur Andersen, 20

Asch, Solomon, 49

Aspen Institute Business Leaders' Dialogue, 19–20

Australia, 4, 25–26

Austria, 109

Averbuch, Tova, 79, 81–82, 84–85

Azriel, Azriel, 85

ba (intentional place), 122

balance, 53–56, 81–82, 100, 102, 138

Balasubramanian, Gomathy, 61, 64–65, 122–124

Barnum, Jeff, 136

Beck, Ulrich, 64–65

being stuck
    and becoming unstuck, 5, 9, 56, 77, 90–91, 134
    from fear, 82, 83
    through power/love imbalances, 1, 8, 22, 23, 76, 114

Ben Yosef, Shay, 76, 79

Bernal, Ana Teresa, 139–140

"best practice" solutions, 5

Bhavishya Alliance
    background of project, 57–58
    disregard for love, 65–67
    falling under polarization, 67–71
    forced participation in, 62
    inattention to power, 61–62, 64–67
    relationship of participants, 58–61
    resulting in disempowerment, 66

bhavishya (future), 59

Bohm, David, 36

Bøjer, Marianne Mille, 120

Brazil, 106, 107, 113

Breznitz, Shlomo, 88

Buber, Martin, 128

business, 4, 12–13, 18–20, 48, 100

Business Leaders' Dialogue (Aspen), 19–20

Canada, 22–23, 25, 115–117

capitalism, 12, 20

Carlin, John, 97

Carvajal, Manuel José, 41

Chambers, Edward, 94–95

change lab, 37–38, 60, 122–126. *See also* Bhavishya Alliance; Sustainable Food Lab

Chardin, Pierre Teilhard de, 31

Chender, Michael, 68

child malnutrition, 57–59, 65

clergy/church power, 48

climate change mitigation. *See* mitigating climate change

co-creation
allowing space for, 62, 89, 91, 93, 108, 109
change lab to support, 126
intention in, 135–136
as new mode for social change, 2, 110, 127
scenario building, 16, 38, 41–42, 83, 85, 87–90
three movements of, 38, 60, 105–110, 124, 125
from trusting connections, 108–109
and the U-Process, 37–38

co-presencing, 38, 60, 106–109, 125

co-realizing, 38, 60, 109–110, 125

co-sensing, 38, 60, 105–106, 108, 124, 125

collective creation. *See* co-creation

collective intelligence, 92

collective self-realization, 18, 117, 125

Colom, Álvaro, 44

Colombia, 41–42, 139–140

complex, 5

complexity, emergent approach to, 120–121

conjunctive processes of being, 7–8

connection
in creating new realities, 44, 47, 108–109
as essential, 26, 94, 109
food system epitomizing, 103–104
as part of love, 9, 30
See also unity

conscious consumption, 113

consensus, 49–50, 66, 69

container, 92–93, 99–100, 102, 116–117, 122–126

Côte d'Ivoire, 12

courage, 132–133

creation. *See* co-creation

Cyprus, 78

de Klerk, F. W., 96, 97

degenerative love
denying impact on others, 114
power's role in, 7–9, 39–42, 48, 50, 88
as reinforcing the status quo, 42–47
suppression of self-realization, 48–49

degenerative power
as lacking in love, 7–9, 25–27
power-over as, 16–18, 22–24
power-to disregarding the other, 18–20, 114

Deng Xiaoping, 120

Destino Colombia, 41, 122, 139

Díez, Elena, 35, 42

differentiation, 82, 88

dilemmas, 53–54

dinokeng (place of rivers), 87

Dinokeng workshops
background of, 87–88
part of renewed drive for unity, 99, 100
producing collective intelligence, 92–93, 122, 127
stumbling progress of, 88–91
working with power dynamics in, 94

disempowerment, 62, 66

disillusionment, 87–88

Dodson, Patrick, 25, 26

du Plessis, Morné, 97

dynamic balance, 54, 56

dynamically complex, 5

ecological challenges. *See* mitigating climate change; Sustainable Food Lab

ecosystem destruction, 26

Eisenstadt, Mia, 61, 64–65, 122–124

El Salvador, 44

elitism, 44–46

emergent approach, 118, 120–121, 124, 136

England, 4

Enron, 18–20

falling
    causes of, 57, 75
    containers to prevent, 99
    response to, 71–73, 127, 128
    as state of power and love, 56, 102, 130
    See also Bhavishya Alliance; polarization

family, gender roles, 7

fear, 68, 71, 82–83, 86–87, 132–137

Fieldtrip (jazz trio), 135–136

figure-ground theory, 81–82

Fitzduff, Mari, 108–109

Flowers, Betty Sue, 37

fluidity. *See* walking

Flyvbjerg, Bent, 117–118

Food Lab. *See* Sustainable Food Lab

food production sustainability, 103–104, 107, 110–111

fragmentation, 88, 98–99

frame. *See* container

Franklin, Lars, 34–35

Freire, Paolo, 42

Friedman, Edwin, 66

Fukuyama, Francis, 12

Fuller, Buckminster, 111–113

fullness, 4, 5

Galtung, Johan, 58

Gardner, John, 82

Gelobter, Michel, 23, 134–135

gender roles, 7

generative love
    as empowering others, 31–32, 50
    as expanding intelligence, 32, 34–35
    power in, 7–9, 29–30, 50
    unity in, 36–37

generative power
    connection to self-realization, 12–13
    love as essential to, 7–9
    power-to as, 17, 18, 20
    purposefulness in, 14–15
    unity in, 20, 26–27

generatively complex, 5, 118, 120–121

Generon, 30, 37, 38, 57, 60, 65–71

Geus, Arie de, 13, 53

gifts, 36

Gimian, Jim, 134, 137

Global Leadership Initiative, 38, 49, 57, 60, 70

Gonzalez, Eduardo, 44

Great Britain, 4

Grillo, LeAnne, 135

group dynamics, 64–65, 81–82, 88, 92–96

groupthink, 88, 92

Guatemala, 17, 32–38, 42–47

Haines, Mark, 20

Hale, Charles, 45–46

Hamilton, Hal, 103, 104, 110–111

Hampden-Turner, Charles, 53

Hani, Chris, 97

Haramati, Avner, 75, 77, 79, 86

Hassan, Zaid, 24, 61, 64–65, 92, 122–124, 136–137

Head, Bob, 87

healing, 130–134

health sector, 48

Heschel, Abraham Joshua, 81

Hill, Julia Butterfly, 26

Hillman, James, 48

Hinkelammert, Franz, 46
homogenization, 82, 83, 85, 88, 100
hope, 88, 136–137
Houston, 18, 19, 23, 122
Howard, John, 26

imbalance, 75, 81–83, 85–87, 100, 102
imperialism, 4
inclusion, 80, 130
India, 56–60, 70, 127–128. *See also*
    Bhavishya Alliance
individual transformation
    awareness of power and love for,
        129
    essence of, 128, 139
    practicing moving fluidly, 132–139
    through balancing ourselves,
        129–134
individuation, 82. *See also* self-
    realization
innovation, 37, 108
institutions, 100
integration, 82, 83, 85, 100
intelligence, 34
intention, 135–136
interdependence, 5, 8, 44–45,
    103–104, 114
Israel, 56, 75, 83, 86, 88. *See also* Jewish
    Israeli Journey project

Jaworski, Joseph, 31, 36–37, 53, 108
Jaworski, Leon, 36
Jewish Israeli Journey project
    history of previous initiatives,
        76–77
    impact of fear on love-power
        dynamic, 81–82
    logic behind, 75–76
    Open Space approach in, 79–80
    outcome of, 83, 85, 122
    participants in, 77–78
    power in Israel-Palestine case, 77
    self-realization in, 78–80
    two sides of love/power in, 78–81

Johnson, Robert, 9, 32, 87–88, 138
Jones, Van, 26
Jordan, Pallo, 16–17
Jung, Carl, 9, 32, 129

Kahane, Dorothy, 17, 29–30, 35, 47–48
Kanyini (film), 25
Kegan, Robert, 130
Kerr, Brenda, 132
King, Martin Luther, Jr., 8–9, 12, 40

ladinos (mixed ancestry), 45
Larson, Jonathan, 2
Lay, Ken, 18–20
le Roux, Pieter, 14
leadership, 36–37, 66, 111, 127–128,
    138
learning journeys, 106
Lewis, Myrna, 68–70
Liebenberg, Johann, 15
Lockyer, Bill, 19
Long, Michael, 26
love
    defined by Tillich, 2, 30
    definitions from various
        disciplines, 31–32
    as disposition towards another,
        31, 32
    as drive toward unity, 2, 30, 32,
        34–37
    as expanding intelligence, 34
    "falling in love," 87–88
    presupposing original oneness, 81
    relationship to power, 26–27, 50
    in Western culture, 50, 95
    See also degenerative love; genera-
        tive love; power and love dynamic;
        states of power and love
Lukes, Stephen, 17

Macapagal-Arroyo, Gloria, 39
MacFarquar, Larissa, 137
Machado, Antonio, 140

Maira, Arun, 59, 127–128

Mandela, Nelson, 13, 87, 96–98

mandorla, 138–139

Manuel, Trevor, 110

Mattar, Helio, 113

Maturana, Humberto, 32, 34

May, Rollo, 7–8

Mbeki, Thabo, 99

Melchiori, Paola, 7

mitigating climate change
approaches to, 113–115
emergent approach to, 118, 120–121
3E Alliance for, 116–118, 120–122, 125–126, 135–136
UNFCCC negotiations, 114–115

Mkhabela, Ishmael, 94

Mockus, Antanas, 41, 42

Mont Fleur Scenario Exercise, 14–15, 16, 29, 32, 87, 96, 110

Moses (Biblical patriarch), 140

Netherlands, 105

"next practice" solutions, 5

NGO (nongovernmental organization), 58

nonattachment, 136–137

nonviolent social change, 8

Northern Ireland, 108–109

Obama, Barack, 94, 137

O'Brien, Bill, 30–31, 127

Ochaeta, Ronalth, 32, 34, 38

Oman, 86–87

oneness, 80, 81. *See also* unity

Open Space, 79–80, 108, 118

Oshry, Barry, 82

other
in the conjunctive process of being, 7
interdependence with the, 5, 8, 44–45, 103–104, 114
love as disposition towards the, 31, 32

power-over the, 17–18, 22–24
in stakeholder dialogues, 59
suppressed in degenerative love, 49–50

Owen, Harrison, 79

Palestinians, 76, 79, 81, 85, 86

Pappenheim, Shlomo, 85–86, 140

parenting styles, 30

Pastrana, Andrés, 41–42

peace
beyond submissive, 1–2, 8, 77, 114, 115
as giving up, 120
the peace-monger, 66
"taking whole" alternative to, 137

peace-monger, 66

Perlas, Nicanor, 40

Philippines, 39–40, 44

Picasso, Pablo, 136

Pienaar, François, 96

polarization
from failing to recognize dilemma, 57, 67–68
immoral power/powerless morality, 8–9
in individuals, 70, 71, 129
in post-apartheid South Africa, 98–99
recognizing and dealing with, 68–71, 73
in relation to climate change, 114
See also Bhavishya Alliance

politeness, 48

politics, 4, 9, 45–46, 48, 117–118

power
defined by Tillich, 2, 30
as the drive for self-realization, 2, 12–13, 17, 30
importance of acknowledging, 64–65, 137
to mitigate climate change, 115
reacting with rationality, 117–118
relational, 94–95

in Western culture, 95
See also degenerative power; generative power; power and love dynamic; power-over; power-to; states of power and love
Power: A Radical View (Lukes), 17
power and love dynamic
   in community organizing approach, 94–96
   nature of the, 26–27, 50, 138–139
   reconciling the, 9, 53–56, 81–82, 100, 102, 138–139
   two movements of, 124–126
   See also states of power and love
power-over
   in degenerative love, 44–46
   as degenerative power, 16–20, 22–24
   denying interconnectedness, 115
   driving projects/agendas as, 65–67
   inquiry into, 73
   power-to morphing into, 18, 78–79, 115
power-to
   in degenerative love, 18–20, 45, 46, 114
   as disconnected/alienated, 58–59, 114
   as generative power, 17, 18, 20
   inquiry into, 73
   morphing into power-over, 18, 78–79, 115
   Open Space approach and, 79–80
   relational, 94–95
presencing, 37
privilege, 44–45
"problematic situations," 113
projections, 88

racial ambivalence, 46
racism, 45–48
Randall, Bob, 25–26
rationality, 117–118
Rautenberg, Tom, 130

reality, emerging, 118, 120–121, 124, 136
regstellende aksie (right-putting action), 98
relational power, 94–95
Remen, Rachel Naomi, 130, 132
residential schooling (Canada), 22
retreating, 106–108
rheos (flow; stream), 134
Rifkind, Gabrielle, 92–93
romance, 87–88
Roy, John, 115–117
Royal Dutch Shell, 12, 19, 36, 53, 113

Samper, Ernesto, 41
Sanderson, John, 25
Saxon, Earl, 113–114
scenario building, 16, 38, 41–42, 83, 85, 87–90
Scharmer, Otto, 37, 47, 108
self-healing, 130–134
self-realization
   causing fragmentation/polarization, 98–99
   collective, 18, 117, 125
   importance to unity, 46–47, 62, 91
   leadership allowing for, 138
   and the other, 17–18, 23
   power as drive for, 2, 12–13, 17, 30
   producing power-over, 78–79
   suppressed in degenerative love, 48–49
   See also individual transformation
Senge, Peter, 31, 32, 36, 37, 111
sensing, 37
separation, 36, 81
September 11 attacks, 82–83
shaman, 132
Shambhala Institute for Authentic Leadership, 135
Shiva, Vandana, 104
Singh, Manmohan, 59

social challenges
   bringing dynamic balance to, 53–56, 100, 102
   change lab structure for, 121–126
   complexity in, 5, 113–114, 118, 120–121
   current mode of addressing, 1–2, 8–9
   important role of power in, 38–39
   interaction of rationality and power, 117–118
   maintaining hope in face of, 88
   role of the individual in, 127–128, 132
   See also being stuck
social change
   balancing/rebalancing in, 83, 85–86, 94
   beginning with leadership, 127–128
   co-realizing in, 38, 60, 109–110, 125
   perspective challenges to, 124
   power and love essential to, 2, 8, 9, 46–47
   progress in, 139–140
   recognizing state of power and love for, 56, 68, 73
   two-movement framing for, 124–126
   U-Process in, 37–38
   See also co-creation; individual transformation
social island. *See* container
socially complex, 5
Society for Organizational Learning (SoL), 31, 32, 38, 86
solo retreats, 106–108
Solving Tough Problems (Kahane), 35, 44, 137
South Africa, 14–18, 23, 29, 30, 47–48, 56, 87–89, 91, 96–100
stakeholder dialogues, 59
states of power and love
   in the individual, 128
   movement within the change lab, 124–126
recognizing for social change, 56, 68, 73
   three, 56, 102, 130
   See also falling; stumbling; walking
status quo, 42–47, 116
"Stolen Generation," 25
Stookey, Crane, 92
structural violence, 58
stuck. *See* being stuck
stumbling
   container for, 92–93, 99–100, 102
   mechanics of, 75, 82
   post-apartheid South Africa, 96–100
   progress made by, 88–91
   righting imbalances, 81–82, 83, 85, 100, 102
   self-correcting individual, 129–134
   See also Dinokeng workshops; Jewish Israeli Journey project
Sun Tzu, 137
Sustainable Food Lab
   change lab work, 105–110, 124, 125
   commitment to systemic change, 110–111, 113, 122, 125–126
   essence of, 104–105
Sweitzer, Susan, 107
Synod of Anglican Bishops, 30
systems thinking, 58, 82

taking whole, 137
Talmud, 140
terra nullius (empty land), 4, 7, 20, 25
Thatcher, Margaret, 12
Theory U, 37–38, 108, 136
Thoreau, Henry David, 11
3E (Economy, Energy, Environment) Alliance, 116–118, 120–122, 125–126, 135–136
Tillich, Paul, 2, 7, 8, 12–13, 17, 26, 30, 32, 46, 54, 81
Tolbert, Bill, 125
tough challenges, 5
Trungpa, Chögyam, 134

U-Process, 37–38, 108, 136
United Nations Framework Convention on Climate Change (UNFCCC), 114–115
United States, post-September 11, 82–83
unity
and acknowledging power, 61–62
assumption of original oneness in, 81
in collective self-realization, 18, 117, 125
creating connections for, 109
fear preventing, 132–133
Jewish Israeli longing for, 80
leadership supporting emergence of, 138
love as drive toward, 2, 30, 32, 34–37, 80
necessity for self-realization in, 46–47, 49–50, 62, 91
as purpose in life, 25–26
recognizing interdependence to achieve, 8
South African drive towards, 96–99
as "taking whole," 137
unhealthy emphasis on, 86–87, 89
unstuck, becoming, 5, 9, 56, 77, 90–91, 134
Uribe, Álvaro, 42

values, balancing contrasting, 54
van der Heijden, Kees, 88, 113
van der Merwe, Louis, 73
Versteegen, Ursula, 22
Visión Guatemala, 32–38, 42–47, 122
walking
change lab for, 121–126

employing an emergent approach, 120–121
leadership change for, 127–128
love redirecting power in, 109
nature of, 103, 140
practicing moving fluidly, 134–139
requiring power to disrupt the status quo, 116–118
through problematic situations, 113
by trusting the parts of the whole, 118
See also mitigating climate change; Sustainable Food Lab
war
beyond aggressive, 8, 77, 114, 115
as giving up, 120
Guatemalan civil, 32, 34, 44–45
"taking whole" alternative, 137
as unworkable solution, 1–2
Weick, Karl, 120–121
Weisbord, Marvin, 69
Wheatley, Margaret, 132
White Planet, The (film), 25, 26
wholeness. *See* unity
Wilkinson, Angela, 108
Wing, Bob, 135
Wizard of Oz (film), 54, 56
Wolfe, Tom, 12
wounds, 130–132
Wouters, Alain, 110

yin and yang, 54

Zalzberg, Ofer, 76–77
Zhou Enlai, 140
Zoughbi, Zoughbi, 39, 40, 100, 102

Reos
About Reos Partners

REOS PARTNERS is an international organization dedicated to supporting and building capacity for innovative collective action in complex social systems.

Reos organizes, designs, and facilitates results-oriented multi-stakeholder change processes with business, government, and civil society organizations. It helps people act together fluidly, in partnership, to address their most vital challenges. Its name comes from the Greek *rheos*, meaning "flow" or "stream."

Reos works with individuals and organizations that want to engage with others to address a particular tough challenge in a complex context where no good maps exist. Reos supports them in convening a team that has diverse perspectives on and stakes in the situation and that is committed to mapping and acting its way forward together. Reos works with this team as they deepen their shared understanding of the realities they wish to affect, clarify their collective intention, and implement initiatives that create new realities.

Reos helps teams produce four types of practical results. They construct new insights about their problematic situation (including their own role in this situation) and new high-leverage options to shift it. They form new relationships with other stakeholders. They build their capacities to effect change. Out of these insights, relationships, and capacities, they take actions that address their challenges.

Reos is known both for its influential contributions to theory and practice, and for the results it has helped to create in the most challenging of contexts. The organization has offices in Cambridge (Massachusetts), Johannesburg, London, San Francisco, and São Paulo.

www.reospartners.com/powerandlove

About the Author
and the Artist

ADAM KAHANE is a partner in the Cambridge, Massachusetts, office of Reos Partners. He is also an Associate Fellow of the Institute for Science, Innovation and Society at the University of Oxford's Saïd Business School.

Adam is a leading organizer, designer, and facilitator of processes through which business, government, and civil society leaders work together to address their toughest, most complex challenges. He has worked in this way in more than fifty countries, in every part of the world, with executives and politicians, generals and guerrillas, civil servants and trade unionists, community activists and United Nations officials, clergy and artists.

During the early 1990s, Adam was head of Social, Political, Economic and Technological Scenarios for Royal Dutch Shell in London. Previously he held strategy and research positions with Pacific Gas and Electric Company (San Francisco), the Organisation for Economic Cooperation and Development (Paris), the International Institute for Applied Systems Analysis (Vienna), the Institute for Energy Economics (Tokyo), and the Universities of British Columbia, California, Toronto, and the Western Cape.

In 1991 and 1992, Adam facilitated the Mont Fleur Scenario Project, in which a diverse group of South African leaders worked together to contribute to their country's transition to democracy.

Since then he has led many such seminal cross-sectoral dialogue-and-action processes, around the world. He was featured in *Fast Company*'s first annual "Who's Fast," and he is a member of the Aspen Institute's Business Leaders' Dialogue, the Commission on Globalisation, Global Business Network, the Global Leadership Network, the Society for Organizational Learning, and the World Academy of Art and Science.

Adam has a BSc in Physics (First Class Honors) from McGill University (Montreal), an MA in Energy and Resource Economics from the University of California (Berkeley), and an MA in Applied Behavioral Science from Bastyr University (Seattle). He has also studied negotiation at Harvard Law School and cello performance at Institut Marguerite-Bourgeoys.

Adam and his wife Dorothy live with their family in Cape Town and Montreal.

kahane@reospartners.com

JEFF BARNUM is a partner in the San Francisco office of Reos Partners. He works with business, government, and cultural leaders on international, national, and local social innovation initiatives. He is a facilitator and process designer and a practicing artist in various media. For him, Reos Partners' work is an extension of Joseph Beuys' notion of "social sculpture," a participatory activity that strives to structure and shape society.

In 1993, Jeff completed a BA in Art and Art History at Rice University (Houston) and in 2003, an MA in Fine Arts from Maine College of Arts (Portland). His academic work focused on building practical and philosophical bridges between creativity and social entrepreneurship.

Between earning those degrees, Jeff worked in various startups and trades and focused on raising his family, studying, and developing his art practice. He traveled internationally, living in Germany, the Netherlands, and Slovenia, and working for several institutes dedicated to social change. Together with IDRIART (the Institute for the Development of Intercultural Relations through the Arts) and its leader Miha Pogacnik, Jeff designed and hosted learning festivals focused on the intersection of business and artistic creativity. He worked with youth from all over the world and facilitated a project to build bridges between Bosnian and Serbian teens.

Jeff and his wife Louisa live in Northern California with their daughters Farranika and Iren.

barnum@reospartners.com

www.jeffbarnum.com

Berrett–Koehler
Publishers

Berrett-Koehler is an independent publisher dedicated to an ambitious mission: *Creating a World That Works for All*.

We believe that to truly create a better world, action is needed at all levels—individual, organizational, and societal. At the individual level, our publications help people align their lives with their values and with their aspirations for a better world. At the organizational level, our publications promote progressive leadership and management practices, socially responsible approaches to business, and humane and effective organizations. At the societal level, our publications advance social and economic justice, shared prosperity, sustainability, and new solutions to national and global issues.

A major theme of our publications is "Opening Up New Space." Berrett-Koehler titles challenge conventional thinking, introduce new ideas, and foster positive change. Their common quest is changing the underlying beliefs, mindsets, institutions, and structures that keep generating the same cycles of problems, no matter who our leaders are or what improvement programs we adopt.

We strive to practice what we preach—to operate our publishing company in line with the ideas in our books. At the core of our approach is stewardship, which we define as a deep sense of responsibility to administer the company for the benefit of all of our "stakeholder" groups: authors, customers, employees, investors, service providers, and the communities and environment around us.

We are grateful to the thousands of readers, authors, and other friends of the company who consider themselves to be part of the "BK Community." We hope that you, too, will join us in our mission.

A BK Currents Book

This book is part of our BK Currents series. BK Currents books advance social and economic justice by exploring the critical intersections between business and society. Offering a unique combination of thoughtful analysis and progressive alternatives, BK Currents books promote positive change at the national and global levels. To find out more, visit **www.bkconnection.com**.

Berrett–Koehler
Publishers

A community dedicated to creating
a world that works for all

Visit Our Website: www.bkconnection.com

Read book excerpts, see author videos and Internet movies, read
our authors' blogs, join discussion groups, download book apps, find
out about the BK Affiliate Network, browse subject-area libraries of
books, get special discounts, and more!

Subscribe to Our Free E-Newsletter, the *BK Communiqué*

Be the first to hear about new publications, special discount offers,
exclusive articles, news about bestsellers, and more! Get on the list
for our free e-newsletter by going to **www.bkconnection.com**.

Get Quantity Discounts

Berrett-Koehler books are available at quantity discounts for orders
of ten or more copies. Please call us toll-free at (800) 929-2929 or
email us at **bkp.orders@aidcvt.com**.

Join the BK Community

BKcommunity.com is a virtual meeting place where people from
around the world can engage with kindred spirits to create a world
that works for all. **BKcommunity.com** members may create their own
profiles, blog, start and participate in forums and discussion groups,
post photos and videos, answer surveys, announce and register for
upcoming events, and chat with others online in real time. Please join
the conversation!